# Finding Angels
# in Boulders

# Finding Angels in Boulders

## An Interfaith Discussion
*on* Dying *and* Death

**BRUCE G. EPPERLY & LEWIS D. SOLOMON**

**CHALICE** PRESS
ST. LOUIS, MISSOURI

Biblical quotations, unless otherwise noted, are from the *New Revised Standard Version Bible,* copyright 1989, Division of Christian Education of the National Council of the Churches of Christ in the United States of America. Used by permission. All rights reserved.

Cover Image: Getty Images
Cover design: Elizabeth Wright
Interior design: Hui-Chu Wang
Art direction: Elizabeth Wright

This book is printed on acid-free, recycled paper.

Visit Chalice Press on the World Wide Web at
www.chalicepress.com

10  9  8  7  6  5  4  3  2  1          05   06   07   08   09

## Library of Congress Cataloging-in-Publication Data

Epperly, Bruce Gordon.
  Finding angels in boulders : an interfaith discussion on dying and death / Bruce G. Epperly and Lewis D. Solomon.
     p. cm.
  ISBN-13: 978-0-827210-36-1 (pbk. : alk. paper)
  ISBN-10: 0-827210-36-1
  1. Death—Religious aspects—Christianity. I. Solomon, Lewis D. II. Title.
  BT825.E678 2004
  248.8'66—dc22

                                                                2004014951

Printed in the United States of America

*We dedicate this book
to spiritual and life partners,*

*Katherine Gould Epperly and Janet Stern Solomon*

# Contents

# A Word of Thanks

As we complete the third volume of this trilogy on progressive Jewish-Christian spirituality, we are again reminded of the ecology of relationships that brought this book into being. We remember those persons whose love and faith has nurtured us from our births and throughout our lives. Healing and wholeness arise out of our experience of relatedness with the gentle movements of the Holy Adventure, embodied in friends, family, and spiritual mentors. Life in its fullness is grounded in the gratitude that comes from affirming and embracing the graceful love we have received through the years.

We would, above all, like to thank our wives, Katherine Gould Epperly and Janet Stern Solomon. They have been spiritual partners, supporters, and inspirations to excellence in our work and in our lives. I, Bruce, am grateful for the encouragement of my son Matthew and mother-in-law Maxine Gould, as well as a handful of spiritual friends who have inspired and challenged me as a spiritual leader and person of faith.

We are grateful to Rabbi Harold White, who has embodied the spirit of Shalom in his three decades of leadership in Jewish-Christian relationships and interfaith dialogue. We are also grateful to David Polk for his support and gentle editorial work. I, Bruce, am thankful for David's editorial support since 1991 and his commitment to quality work in process-relational theology.

We dedicate this book to all those who wish to follow the Holy Adventure in new and surprising ways.

# CHAPTER ONE

## *Finding Angels in Boulders*

Once upon a time, a neighbor observed the sculptor Michelangelo rolling a boulder up the hillside to his front porch. When the sculptor took out his hammer and began pounding on the jagged rock, his neighbor was overcome with curiosity.

"What are you doing, hammering on that boulder?" he asked. The sculptor replied, "There's an angel inside, and I'm trying to let it out."

The story of Michelangelo and the boulder describes our encounter with the reality of death. At first glance, a jagged and misshapen boulder seems an unlikely hiding place for an angel. Its jagged exterior can cut and bruise the careless climber. To the untrained eye, a boulder seems bereft of beauty and promise. At best, it is a nuisance. At worst, it is a threat. An avalanche of boulders can block a mountain trail, making the path ahead impassable or perilous, or cover the entrance of a cave, trapping miners inside. But to the artist, a boulder or rough-hewn stone can be thing of wonder and beauty. To the creative imagination, the unpromising exterior may hide a

1

diamond or a work of art. To the holy imagination, angels spring forth in the most unlikely situations.

Death, in its many dimensions, is the ultimate boulder that blocks our path to the future. As we ponder our own mortality and the deaths of our loved ones, we can identify with the women who came to Jesus' tomb on Easter morning. As they walked hopelessly to the tomb of their teacher Jesus, hoping to anoint his body as a sign of their respect and love for him, they asked each other, "Who will roll away the stone for us from the entrance to the tomb?" (Mk. 16:3). To the women who followed the healer Jesus, the boulder symbolized the ultimate finality of death in all its manifestations. Death had been victorious—their beloved friend was gone forever. Only memory and grief remained. A jagged stone blocked the way to the future, breaking their hearts and demolishing their hopes. In their despondence, they could not imagine any power that could roll away the stone and make a path to the future.

## Finding Hope in Hopeless Situations

Death and grief cannot be escaped. Indeed, they are as essential to life as birth, childhood adventure, romance, and maturity. Still, death strikes terror in our hearts. Even persons of faith are profoundly disoriented at the prospect of their own or imminent mortality. Abandoned by his closest followers, Jesus cries out, "my God, my God, why have you forsaken me" as he endures the pain and humiliation of the cross.

Centuries before, the author of Psalm 22 described his own disorientation at the prospect of abandonment and death. Perhaps the psalmist once believed that death and debilitation were the fate of others—something that could never happen to him—until his complacency was shattered by the onset of illness, searing pain, failure, and depression. When he cried out for a compassionate friend and a loving God, he was met with silence and absence. But still he hopes against hope that he will find a blessing amid the brokenness of body, mind, and spirit he felt.

My God, my God, why have you forsaken me?
> Why are you so far from helping me, from the
> > words of my groaning?

O my God, I cry by day, but you do not answer;
> and by night, but find no rest.

Yet you are holy,
> enthroned on the praises of Israel.

In you our ancestors trusted;
> they trusted and you delivered them....

My hands and feet have shriveled;

I can count all my bones.

(Ps. 22:1–4, 16b–17a)

Authentic spirituality embraces the totality of life. While some persons identify spirituality solely with success and well-being, the spiritual journey encompasses darkness and light, failure and success, sickness and health, absence and presence. Healthy spirituality enables us to experience the Holy One in all the seasons of life, especially in life's painful inevitabilities.

C. S. Lewis notes that the great religions of the world emerged before the discovery of painkillers. Though we may eliminate many illnesses and provide comfort to the sick and dying, Lewis' insight still speaks to the inevitability of suffering, death, and grief. We cannot avoid life's most jagged boulders, but we may discover an angel in life's most desperate situations.

Honest spirituality seeks to never romanticize death. Death is no illusion. Though our spirits may be liberated from the burdens of body, mind, and spirit with our final breaths, the pains of death are real. The price of eternal life is physical death! Even the most gentle spiritual midwifery cannot eliminate pain, whether it be at life's beginning or end. Just walk through the hallways of an oncology clinic. Hope and fear are written on each face. We pray for a cure and trust the skills of physicians and complementary health care givers. Nevertheless, we fear helplessness, loneliness, vulnerability, and pain. Despite our faith, we may still have doubts about our destiny beyond the grave. Who will be with us in the darkness of death? Who will we be at the moment when we breathe our last breath—will we simply evaporate into non-being or will we be welcomed with open arms and gentle light at the next stage of our journey?

During the course of writing this book, Bruce's father Everett died at the age of 91. Following a severe stroke, he was confined to a wheelchair and bed for the final five years of his life. Though a man of deep faith, the impact of the stroke made it impossible for him to read scripture or vocalize his prayers. Only with great effort on the part of his friends could he attend church at Christmas and Easter. Still, he rejoiced in visits from his children and friends from church. Despite a profound hearing loss, his heart was warmed when his pastor Michael-Ray Mathews and his social worker Sally Hedman sang the old hymns of faith to him. No one can romanticize the indignities of wearing a diaper or being hoisted up like dead weight by the caring and attentive nursing staff. Life was difficult for this gentle and unassuming man. Often, Bruce and his brother left the nursing home with broken hearts as their father, the man who once had been their protector and guide, now begged them to take him home.

Following his father's funeral, one of Bruce's friends shared a story from Everett Epperly's last months. As he leaned to say good-bye to Bruce's father, he heard Everett say with a melancholy expression, "I'm stuck." Then, after a moment's pause, Everett's expression changed. A slight smile appeared on his face as he finished the sentence, "But that's ok."

Elisabeth Kübler-Ross, in the same spirit, once noted, "I'm not ok. You're not ok. But it's ok!" The only spirituality that matters—the only spiritual path we can trust—embraces death with the same honesty as it embraces celebration and success. Because all of us, even the most fortunate, will eventually be "stuck"—grieving at the graveside or helplessly awaiting our own deaths. Because we must pass through the valley of the shadow of death, we need a faith and a God for the wintry times as well as for the warmth of summer.

## A Faith of Sufficient Stature

The complexities of living and dying require a complex and inclusive faith and an equally complex and inclusive vision of God. The biblical tradition proclaims that Jesus grew in "wisdom and stature." Like us, Jesus needed to grow in experiencing and understanding the God of his Hebraic parents. As the spiritual children of Abraham and Sarah, Isaiah, Jesus and Mary, the quest for wisdom and stature is also our calling as progressive Jews and Christians. Our progressive spirituality challenges us to become pilgrims of transformation and inclusion as we share in God's Holy Adventure.[1]

Wisdom is the intuition of holiness and beauty in ordinary life. While we appropriately celebrate the dramatic events of our lives and faith traditions—the birth of a child, our wedding day, Passover and the exodus, Good Friday and Easter—wisdom reminds us that God is present in the ordinary and often unnoticed events of life. God is by our side as we prepare lunches for school, soothe a frightened child, or touch a friend at a funeral. Faith may be inspired by dramatic moments of new birth and transformation, but it is also nurtured by everyday acts of kindness and devotion. The God who creates the universe moment by moment is present in the birthing of each child and each cell. The God who breathes upon the dust, giving life to humankind, is also the God who receives us in our final breaths. The God whose love encircles the powerful also embraces the destitute and downtrodden.

Progressive Jews and Christians affirm the universality of revelation. Every situation—even the most adverse—gives witness of God's presence. God's wisdom inspires the paleontologist and the surgeon as well as the holistic healer and poet. We can "taste and see God" at the graveside and the emergency room. We can experience God's care in the healing touch of a friend or energy worker and in the medications we take. The power of the exodus and the resurrection as stories of faith is found not just in their uniqueness, but also in their universality. The ever-present God seeks liberation and new life for all creation.

Progressive Jews and Christians also affirm a God of stature, who challenges us to become persons of stature. Theologian Bernard Loomer spoke of "stature" as the most important religious virtue. A person of stature embraces as much complexity of experience as possible without losing her or his personal center or integrity. In an age in which popular religious devotion is identified with exclusion and intolerance, spiritual stature looks for the truth wherever it is found. Such devotion rejoices in healing by whatever holy name it has been invoked. Spiritual stature dares to include death as well as life, failure as well as success, doubt as well as belief, as essential elements in the religious journey. Religions of stature proclaim boldly the faith that they affirm, while recognizing the limitations of human belief systems and the presence of God in the other's faith tradition. As progressive Christians, we affirm God's unique presence in Jesus of Nazareth, but also embrace the spiritual wisdom of the Hebraic prophets, Kabbalistic mystics, and contemporary Jewish theologians and philosophers. As progressive Jews, we see God's presence uniquely at work in the history of Israel and its spiritual leaders, but we also recognize God's voice in the words of Jesus and the experiences of Christian mystics and social reformers.

The God we need in life's most challenging moments must also be a God of stature. The God of justice must also be merciful in the quest to transform and heal the oppressor. The God of acceptance and love must also be the source of challenge and unrest. The God of birth must have the stature to embrace and transform death and grief.

Progressive spirituality affirms a vision of reality in which God seeks wholeness for all creation, not merely humankind or our own culture. Dynamic and lively in spirit, progressive Judaism and Christianity assert that we can experience, within the context of our personal and cultural limitations, the Holy Adventure that we call God. In experiencing God's presence in our lives, we find comfort and rest, but also challenge and adventure.

Weaving together faith and practice, progressive Judaism and Christianity provide tools for transformation and prescriptions for wholeness. These transformative religious practices join ancient wisdom and contemplation with contemporary global spirituality, and enable grieving persons to experience comfort, forgiveness, and hope for the future. They also provide spiritual healing when a physical cure is no longer possible. As progressive Jews and Christians, we can affirm life in the midst of death and strength amid vulnerability because we are always connected with the Loving Adventure from whom healing, companionship, and comfort emerge.

Spiritual healing does not depend on our efforts, but our openness to the Holy One whose compassion brings hope and possibility. With all our doubts and struggles to discern the Living God, we trust that we will, in living and dying, always remain in God's gentle care.

Our hope is ultimately neither in orthodoxy, for no human can truly know God, nor in enlightenment or perfection, for the ecology of life contributes both health and sickness in each moment's experience. Our trust is in the gentle and loving presence who empowers us to be companions in healing the sick and comforting the dying, and whose loving care promises growth and life now and forever in the Great Mystery that lies ahead. Our trust is in the one who provides spiritual freedom even when we are stuck in the mire of sickness, disability, and death.

Martin Buber tells the story of a legendary Hasidic teacher:

> After the maggid's death, his disciples came together and talked about the things he had done. When it was Rabbi Schneur Zalman's turn, he asked them, "Do you know why our master went to the pond every day at dawn and stayed there for a little while before coming home again?"
>
> They did not know why. Rabbi Zalman continued: "He was learning the song with which the frogs praise God. It takes a very long time to learn that song."[2]

This is our goal as well: to truly listen to the voices of the dying and our own fears of death; to hear the voice of that which is most mysterious and voiceless within ourselves and in the universe; to discern the melody of Eternal Life in the passing moment and the dying day. As you share the journey of progressive spirituality on the pathways of death and grief, we pray that as you listen, you will hear the Divine whisper in your life's most unexpected and distressing events and that you will discover Eternal Life in life's most transitory moments.

# CHAPTER TWO

# Adventures in Immortality

When Sharon retired from a lifetime of high school teaching, she was ecstatic. "Now, I can study, write, and travel. Maybe, my husband and I can buy a cottage in Tuscany." Just a month later, she was diagnosed with liver cancer. At first, she was overwhelmed by the news. The only image of the dying process that Sharon could remember was her own mother's painful and lonely death from liver cancer. She remembered how her mother was imprisoned by a conspiracy of silence that left her a passive victim of mysterious powers beyond her control. Her first response was to shudder fearfully at the knowledge that her odds of survival were only slightly better than her mother's had been a decade before. But despite her fear of the future, Sharon was determined to take another path—I will live consciously, vitally, and wholeheartedly until the day I die, whenever that may be.

As she began her first round of chemotherapy, Sharon affirmed to her family and her friends, "I'm not planning to die yet. All of my life, I've lived adventurously. I'm not going to stop now. I don't know how many years or months I have ahead of me, but I'm going to live each day to its fullest. Each day will be a new adventure." Throughout her teaching career, Sharon's mind had been her best friend. Her life was one long adventure of ideas. Now, she was going to put her intellectual powers to work again. She researched complementary as well as Western medical approaches to cancer. She also began a disciplined program of yoga, visualization exercises, meditation, and spiritual affirmations. During her chemotherapy, she repeated spiritual affirmations and imaged the healing light infusing her body along with the chemotherapy. Her spiritual affirmations were simple and direct:

> I choose life every day.
> God gives me the courage to face cancer.
> I ask for help whenever I need it.
> I share my wisdom with my family and friends.
> I am a partner with my health care givers.
> I am in God's hands regardless of the outcome.

Sharon's affirmations were antidotes to fear and depression. They reminded her that while death was real, it was not the *only* reality. God's Eternal Spirit would sustain her in all things.

In the four years Sharon survived after the initial diagnosis, she claimed the holiness of each moment. Although she did not regularly attend services at the temple, she reclaimed her Jewish spiritual heritage, especially the wisdom of the Psalms and the mysticism of the Kabbalah. She arose each morning with the psalmist's praise, "this is the day that God has made, I will rejoice and be glad in it" (Ps. 118:24). Whenever she felt alone and afraid, Sharon turned to a simple breath prayer, imagining that with each breath, she was inhaling the love of God. Sharon chose to let the Divine light shine through her to embrace her children, grandchildren, former colleagues and students, and husband. Sharon lived a lifetime in her final four years. She even spent a season in Tuscany, sharing a villa with her husband and visiting friends and family. Her living and dying was a witness to the biblical affirmation that "love is as strong as death" (Song 8:6). Her dying was a living adventure in immortality!

## Embracing Mortality

Despite the advances of modern medicine, the mortality rate remains 100 percent. The irony of our mortality is captured in the words of a whimsical bumper sticker:

Eat sensibly.
Exercise regularly.
Don't smoke or drink to an excess.
And die anyway!

Given the trauma of dying and bereavement, author C. S. Lewis wonders if Jesus did any favors for Lazarus and his sisters Mary and Martha when he raised Lazarus from the dead. Now, Lazarus would have to die twice! While we may eliminate certain diseases, we will never be able to eliminate death itself. To our dismay, our greater longevity creates problems of its own—chronic illness, Alzheimer's disease, prostate cancer, arthritis, rising health care costs, and financial woes.

In its quest for technological solutions to life's most basic issues, the modern world has often denied the reality of death with euphemism and silence. But death will not go away. Our modern denial of death has made death all the more fearful and complicated as physicians and family members find little spiritual guidance for the care of the dying and virtually no insight for responding to the profound religious and ethical issues raised by the universality of death. In the modern world, death has become, in the words of psychiatrist Robert Jay Lifton, a "lost season." We have forgotten that although the confrontation with death can destroy a person, it can also inspire us to rejoice in the wonder of life and reach out to others in love. Our living and dying can be an adventure in immortality in which we embrace the birth and death of each passing moment.

Death is the final frontier, but there is hope on the horizon. Steeped in the biblical tradition of exodus and resurrection, our spiritual traditions invite us to live and die adventurously. We see the same spirit of liberation, healing, and new life in the growing partnership of physicians and spiritual leaders. Thanks to the pioneering work of Elisabeth Kübler-Ross, issues of death and dying have come out of the closet and become themes of books, movies, symposia, ethical discussions, spiritual practices, and medical school courses. Hospices have become spiritual homes for pilgrims on their final journey. At these way stations for persons on life's final adventure, comfort care has replaced aggressive technology in responding to the needs of persons with terminal illnesses. In their final days, persons find comfort and empowerment through a creative synthesis of pain medication, pastoral care and spiritual direction, complementary care modalities such as therapeutic and reiki healing touch, and the companionship of friends.

Still, despite the hope for survival after death affirmed by the Jewish and Christian spiritual traditions, most of us do our best to avoid thinking about the grim reaper. We act as if the famous syllogism from college philosophy classes applies to Socrates and other persons, but surely not to ourselves:

All humans are mortal.
Socrates is human.
Therefore, Socrates is mortal.

Yet in spite of our denial, death is our companion every step of the way. In befriending our deaths, we may also embrace our lives in their brevity and wonder. On the frontier where life and death meet, our faith tells us that God has something more in store for each one of us. The one who loved us into life will also receive us with open arms and a loving touch when we breathe our final breath.

## Thinking about Death

When you think of the word "death," what initially comes to mind? How do you feel when you think of the potential death of your spouse, child or children, parent, or an intimate friend? Now, how do you feel when you think of your own death? With Leo Tolstoy's character Ivan Illych, we may find ourselves asking, "Where will I be when I am no more?" At the hour of our death, will we fall into nothingness or be greeted by the loving embrace of the Holy One? What is our image of our future and the future of our loved ones beyond the grave?

While one philosopher noted that continuously thinking about death is as hazardous to your mental health as looking continuously at the sun is hazardous to your eyesight, it is impossible to live courageously, compassionately, and adventurously apart from a creative encounter with our mortality. Yet as we face the inevitability of death, we need a worldview and vision of human possibility that integrates both life and death, and constancy and change. We need to find a way to affirm the constancy of life even as we accept the finality of death. With the Christian reformer Martin Luther, we recognize that healing and wholeness involves affirming the reality of death as well as the hope for eternity: "In the midst of life, we are surrounded by death. But in the midst of death, we are surrounded by life."

Healthy spirituality awakens us to the possibility of finding a blessing in our brokenness and a healing in that which cannot be cured. Every moment can be a window into God's Holy Adventure. The death we fear and the grief that haunts us can also awaken us to the deeper movements of Divine Grace in our lives. Experiencing hope in the present finds its source in a hopeful vision of reality and the destiny of ourselves and those we love.

## Hope beyond the Grave

After decades of denying the possibility of the afterlife, progressive Christians and Jews are now exploring adventurous visions of life after death. These postmortem visions challenge our imagination and open the door to personal spiritual transformation. They invite us to revise our maps of reality even though we cannot fully imagine the future that lies ahead for us. They call us to live adventurously in this life as well.

In the last thirty years, researchers are discovering what mystics have known all along—that the boundary between life and death is permeable. Researchers, such as Raymond Moody, describe "near death experiences"—those surprising adventures in which persons, temporarily pronounced dead, embark on timeless journeys down tunnels of light which include encounters with "deceased" friends and relatives, a life review, and encounters with Spiritual Beings, often identified as God or Jesus. Upon returning home from these unexpected adventures, these pilgrims no longer fear what lies beyond the grave. Their current lives are transformed as well. This lifetime is now experienced through the lens of eternity—as part of an everlasting journey that calls us to live each moment with joy, intimacy, and love. Like mystics of all ages and faiths, these adventurers discover that time and space take on new meaning. Ordinary acts, such as preparing a child's lunch or carpooling to work, become icons of Divinity.[1]

Other researchers, such as psychiatrist Brian Weiss, ponder the possibility of "past life experiences."[2] Under hypnosis, persons have discovered relationships between the challenges of this lifetime and experiences from one or more previous lifetimes. In therapeutic contexts, these prenatal adventurers explore connections between their current fears and anxieties and the pain of the past. They may also discover a relationship between their current gifts and talents and experiences that occurred long before their current lifetimes.

Whether these past life reflections point to the reality of past lives or to an intimate, though unconscious, connectedness with deceased humans from other generations, past life experiences, along with near death experiences, suggest that our current lives are part of a much greater cosmic adventure. We are shaped by the totality of the human, planetary, and cosmic history. We come from God and return to God, and in the meantime, God is our earthly companion. Still, even those persons who have gained insight and peace from mystic encounters with the Eternal must face their own mortality. Though their compasses are pointed toward eternity, they must eventually embark on the journey through the valley of the shadow of death. Like the rest of us, these adventurers must let go of the beauties of this life and the ties of love in order to embrace the wonders of the next. Yet their adventures remind us that here and now, in this moment, our lives are grounded in the eternal love of an adventurous God.

## Between Time and Eternity

Our spiritual parents lived in constant awareness of mortality. Life was brief and often brutal. Long before astronomers and physicists intuited the vastness of the universe, the ancients recognized the brevity of life and the apparent insignificance of our earthly adventure. They lived hopefully between swiftly moving time and the trustworthiness of the Eternal. In the words of the psalmist:

[God], you have been our dwelling place
in all generations.
Before the mountains were brought forth,
or ever you had formed the earth and the world,
from everlasting to everlasting you are God.
You turn us back to dust,
and say, "Turn back, you mortals."
For a thousand years in your sight
are like yesterday when it is past,
or like a watch in the night.
You sweep them away; they are like a dream,
like grass that is renewed in the morning;
in the morning it flourishes and is renewed;
in the evening it fades and withers.
(Ps. 90:1–6)

Jesus of Nazareth captured that same image of life's brevity with his words from the Sermon on the Mount:

> Consider the lilies of the field, how they grow; they neither toil nor spin, yet I tell you, even Solomon in all his glory was not clothed like one of these. But if God so clothes the grass of the field, which is alive today and tomorrow is thrown into the oven, will he [God] not much more clothe you—you of little faith? (Mt. 6:28b–30)

Our earthly lives are brief, but God is eternal, and in God's eternity, we find hope at life's edges. As we view the vastness of time and space, we confess with the author of Psalm 8:

> When I look at your heavens, the work of your fingers,
>     the moon and the stars that you have established;
> what are human beings that you are mindful of them,
>     mortals that you care for them? (Ps. 8:3–4)

However, in encountering the God whose love gives eternity to perpetually perishing creaturely life, we can joyfully affirm:

> Yet you have made them a little lower than God,
>     and crowned them with glory and honor. (Ps. 8:5)

Beyond our experiences of dislocation and anxiety, there is the enduring reality of God's loving creativity. We are children of the Eternal even as we live fleetingly and then perish on this swiftly moving planet.

## Spiritual Truths for Adventurous Dying

The holistic spirituality of the biblical tradition embraces the totality of life. The realities of life and death find their meaning in a lively and dynamic vision of reality, grounded in the affirmation of God's intimate care for all creation.

*The first great truth of biblical spirituality is the reality of change.* Life is a perpetual arising and perishing. One moment dies only to give birth to another. Death and rebirth are the nature of life. Even God is constantly changing. Like the wind whipping over the Sea of Galilee and Mount Sinai, God ceaselessly gives life to all things and constantly transforms the Divine relationship to humankind. God's eternal spirit weaves together constancy and change. There is a time for everything under heaven—"a time to be born and a time to die" (Ecc. 3:2). Faithful companionship with God involves letting go of the past and venturing forth into the future toward which the Divine lures us. Change and death characterize each moment as well as our final departure from this lifetime.

*The second great truth of our lives is that our unique and transitory lives matter—now and for eternity.* Each moment perishes, but lives forever in the Divine memory and in its impact on planetary history. Healthy religion balances the lures of the afterlife with the immediacy of the present moment. This life is no illusion, but a precious opportunity to love God in the world of the flesh. Our choices can make the difference between life and death, and health and illness for ourselves and the planet. We can be God's partners in mending the world.

*Biblical spirituality affirms a third great truth, the intimate relationship of this life and the next.* Progressive Christianity and Judaism affirm a continuity of experience and identity between this life and the next. Our postmortem existence embraces and transforms our current lifetime in its fullness. How we treat others—our love, forgiveness, and justice in this life—is a factor in both their and our own afterlives. We create, to some extent, our eternity by our thoughts, deeds, and words today! We can bring beauty or ugliness to our own and others' futures in this life and the next. To believe in survival after death plunges us deeper into caring for this world. Affirming the eternal destiny of humankind challenges us to seek love and justice in the here and now.

The interplay of time and eternity that characterizes each life is captured in the words of Rabbi Bunam:

Everyone must have two pockets, so that he can reach into one or the other. In the right pocket are the words, "For my sake the world was created," and in the left are the words, "I am earth and ashes."[3]

Our holy adventure in living and dying is revealed in the story is told of two fetuses who were awaiting birth. As they felt the first uterine contractions, they were filled with anxiety about what the future would bring. They asked one another, "is there life outside the womb? Will mother take care of us once we leave the womb or will we be plunged into utter nothingness?" Imagine their surprise and ecstasy, when they emerged from the womb into the loving arms of their mother. The one who had carried them to term would nurture and love them throughout their earthly adventure. She would also receive them with loving arms at their moment of death.

Like these anxious fetuses, we cannot fully imagine what lies beyond the grave. But we live in hope that the Holy Adventure that gives birth to all things will join our earthly adventure with an infinite journey beyond the grave. The love of God weaves together time and eternity and the adventures of this life and the next.

## Living Your Immortality

When you reflect upon the afterlife, what images come to mind? Take a moment to relax and breathe in the spaciousness of life. With each breath, surround yourself the vital and loving presence of the Divine. Experience this Holy Presence embracing you like the arms of a parent, lover, or friend. Let yourself go into the world of God's holy imagination. What do you fear about dying? What concerns, if any, do you have about the afterlife? What images of the afterlife are most compelling to you? Are you alone or are you surrounded by friends and loved ones? Do you experience God's presence in the world beyond? If you had only one possession you could take beyond the grave, what would it be? While we can never fully fathom the mysteries of God or the afterlife, imaginatively exploring our hopes and concerns gives us a starting point for our ultimate earthly adventure. As we experience God's unfettered imagination for ourselves and the universe, we can experience eternal life in a world of change.

Believe it or not, a person can have faith and hope without believing in survival after death. The patriarchs and matriarchs of Judaism and their contemporaries—Abraham, Sarah, Moses—did not expect to experience life after death. As Abraham and Sarah faced their own mortality, they were plunged into deep depression until God gave them a child Isaac to carry on their name and become the parent of a great people. Their hope was in the survival of children who would follow them, keeping their memory alive, and ensuring the impact of their lives on future generations. More than that, however, Abraham, Sarah, and the early Jews, found their hope in the Divine Companion whose love guided them in this life and promised a future for their descendents.

Even if we believe in survival after death, our sense of meaning and joy in the present is grounded in the significance of our lives for future generations. Zest and adventure, commitment and hope, are founded on the trust that although what we do moment by moment will eventually perish, the impact of our lives is everlasting. If the future holds no promise, we are tempted merely to eat, drink, and be merry and to exploit the ecosystem solely for our own benefit. As we look at the human adventure, we want to survive beyond the grave, but we also want this lifetime to contribute to the well being of future generations. We want to live on in the genes, dreams, and actions of our children, students, coworkers, and countless persons shaped by our lives. More than that, we hope that this life is treasured by the Divine Companion, the Loving One whose tender care insures that nothing of value is ever lost. Even if the ravages of Alzheimer's destroy our memory and sense of self, there is One who will not forget, whose love embraces the smallest step and the greatest achievement.

Can you imagine the wondrous possibility that your life is your unique gift to God—that everything you think, do, and feel, shapes the Divine experience? Because you exist, the Holy One is a different kind of God and the universe is a different reality. Jews and Christians alike marvel each Christmas season at reruns of "It's a Wonderful Life." More than nostalgia or sentimentality, the adventures of George Bailey remind us that each one of us, however insignificant our lives may seem, is necessary to the universe and our human companions. In the dynamic matrix of life, our lives are unrepeatable. Though we may doubt the significance of our lives, the contemporary scientific image of "the butterfly effect" reminds us that even the smallest of acts can make the difference between life and death, health and illness, for ourselves and others.

In light of the eternal impact of our actions and the relationship between this life and the next, what kind of world are you creating? What gift do you want to give to the universe? What kind of world do you want to give to God? The mortality of all flesh challenges us to compassion and ethical integrity.

In reflecting on the interplay of time and eternity, Rabbi Abraham Joshua Heschel asserted that:

> The greatest problem is not how to continue, but how to exalt our existence. The cry for life beyond the grave is presumptuous, if there is no cry for eternal life prior to our descending to the grave. Eternity is not perpetual future but perpetual presence. He has planted in us the seed of eternal life. The world to come is not only the hereafter but also a *herenow*. The deepest wisdom man can attain is to know his destiny is to aid, to serve…This is the meaning of death: the ultimate self-dedication to the divine. Death so understood will not be distorted by the craving for immortality, for this act of giving away is reciprocity on man's part for God's gift of life. For the pious man it is a privilege to die.[4]

We hope for immortality. But the gift of the future finds its meaning in gratitude and service to the Holy One. In our own thanksgiving for the gift of life and the opportunity to create, we commit ourselves to contributing something of beauty to the present and future lives of our companions in God's Holy Adventure.

## Images of Hope at the Edges of Life

When most Christians imagine survival after death, they envisage the stark chasm between heaven and hell. Heaven is a place where angels recline on clouds, playing harps before the Almighty. The heavenly inhabitants enjoy endless bliss in a realm where the streets are paved with gold. Hell is an unending inferno, the destination of anyone who has turned her or his back on God and God's Son. Perhaps, however, things are more complicated than these popular images and the descriptions given by televangelists and fundamentalist Christians.

In Bruce's small town Baptist church, the qualifications for heaven and hell were clear. To secure a heavenly home, it was only necessary to: believe that Jesus is your savior, trust the Bible as God's word, get baptized by immersion (dipped all the way under the water), and be obedient to biblical principles. Hell was the destiny of anyone who did not follow that narrow path: the non-Christian, the unbaptized pagan, and, ironically, liberal Christians whose concept of Divine mercy led them to deny the existence of eternal damnation! How simplistic and individualistic this traditional viewpoint actually was! Bruce's fellow worshippers could not fathom the complexities of belief and unbelief: how a person's family of origin, mental state, life experiences, and chemical balance, could shape our ability to believe in God or formulate certain images of the Divine.

The imperialistic dogma of this conservative Christianity asserted that the most fallible mortal could smugly claim a place in the promised land that was denied to persons like Socrates, Gandhi and Buddha simply because they never encountered Jesus or affirmed a particular confession of faith. Though they spoke of God's love and forgiveness of sins, God only loved those whose faith reflected doctrinal orthodoxy. At the moment of their deaths, God abandoned them to their rightful punishment. Death was the ultimate limit on Divine patience, love, and interest in these lost souls. Bruce's Baptist companions could not conceive that the goal of a Loving God in the afterlife might be healing and transformation rather than punishment and damnation, even for those who had not consciously known the Holy One in this lifetime.

Today, many persons who grew up, like Bruce, in such theological environments recognize that such images of God and the afterlife are too cramped and narrow-minded to address the complexity of human experience and our pluralistic age. If God is so arbitrary and unjust, who can really be certain of their own salvation? Can we really love a God whose criterion for eternal bliss or everlasting torment rests simply on the accidents of birth, faith tradition, and family of origin? These images of eternal punishment for wayward souls have driven countless persons from the church and frightened others into accepting Jesus as their savior in order to escape eternal damnation.

***Re-imaging Heaven.*** Progressive Jews and Christians affirm a very different image of survival after death than the popular individualistic pictures of heaven and hell. The reality of connectedness, creativity, adventure, and partnership, characteristic of this life, continues beyond the grave. Biblical images of shalom, the reign of God, and, for Christians specifically, the body of Christ and resurrection, describe human hope in terms of a spiritual community in which peace abounds, tears are transformed into laughter, enemies become friends, and all persons experience wholehearted love of God and one another. In this community of love, individuality is transformed as we claim our true interdependence with all things. In the realm of shalom, we experience our true stature as God's children, whose spirits are spacious, caring, and loving. Our personality is not lost, like a drop of water in the ocean, but is fulfilled in its loving embrace of every other personality. In the ecology of life, death, and immortality, God's unquenchable love will eventually lure each creature toward spiritual completion.

The Christian image of the body of Christ further defines the Messianic Reign of God in terms of an interdependent community in which uniqueness is celebrated and diversity affirmed. This is no "cookie cutter" immortality but a glimmering vision of a spiritual rainbow in which each Divine spark reflects God's light in its own unique way.

In God's Reign, justice is fulfilled, but Divine Justice is shaped by an eternal love that can transform even the most flawed person into someone of beauty in this life and the next. While this process of transformation may be painful in terms of our recognition of the dissonance between what we were and what could have been, the Great Physician's ultimate goal is the healing of every life in this life and the next. God's power in the world is not coercive or punitive, but healing and redemptive.

In God's Messianic Age, the world beyond the grave is characterized by fully loving relationships. For the earliest Christians, this hope was grounded in the resurrection of Jesus and the Hebraic images of the resurrection of the dead and God's dream of shalom. According to the Christian tradition, the crucified Jesus rose on the third day, and became the hope for transformation of the whole person—body, mind, spirit, and relationships—in God's reign of shalom. Affirming the universality of Jesus' resurrection, the early Christians saw it as the affirmation of the hopes of the Jewish people as well as themselves. God is faithful both to the Gentiles and to the Jewish people, and will ultimately bring humankind in its spiritual diversity to healing and fulfillment.

While the resurrection of the dead will always remain a mystery to the rational mind, this radical notion asserts that rebirth and transformation can occur in the most dire situations and that our hope beyond the grave is for something "more," not "less," than our current embodied existence. What we have loved most in the world of the flesh will be recreated and transformed in surprising ways beyond the grave. We will dance and sing, learn and embrace, love and be loved, and grow and explore in an environment where our deepest spiritual desires will find fulfillment and give birth to new adventures in companionship with God.

Whether or not we have literal physical bodies in the afterlife is ultimately irrelevant to the deeper meaning of the resurrection. What we will have is wholeness, adventure, and love. The resurrection of all things, like the resurrection of Jesus, points to the communal nature of the afterlife as the holy unity of mind, body, spirit, and relationships in the dynamic interplay of personal growth and collective transformation. We cannot find wholeness in this life or the next on our own, but only in relationship to the well-being of all creation. Divine love alone is eternal and those who live by love experience everlasting life in this moment and throughout eternity. When the early Christians shouted, "Christ is risen," they affirmed that God has the final word in life and death, and that God can overcome any physical, spiritual, or emotional challenge that confronts us.

The story is told of a man who journeyed for years with his trusted dog as his only companion. He shared his food and bedroll with his aging hound. Now they were on their last pilgrimage, with heaven as their destination. One evening, they arrived at the gates of what appeared to be heaven. When he sought admission, the gatekeeper gladly welcomed the man, until he saw the bedraggled hound. "There's a place for you here, but not for your dog." After a moment's thought, the traveler replied, "Thank you for your offer. But without my trusted friend, there is no heaven for me." Later that evening, he came upon a beautiful city. When they sought entrance, both the pilgrim and his dog were welcomed. "You have found heaven," the gatekeeper stated, "You have passed the final test. Down the road, the gate you passed is hell. If you had abandoned your dog, you would have lost your soul." Only love can transcend the grave, and love embraces all creation in its quest for healing and transformation.

Dualistic images of heaven and hell and reward and punishment are too narrow to embrace our spiritual wingspan. They encourage even faithful persons to abandon those they love to nonexistence—which would be a blessing—or to an eternity of terror and meaninglessness. All of creation longs for fulfillment and will eventually be healed. Everything that is loved, from dogs to dolphins, shares in the Divine Eternity.

In light of the emerging global spirituality, we must also let our imaginations take us beyond the traditional popular Jewish and Christian images of life after death to explore the insights of mystics of all religious traditions. In contrast the dualistic images of heaven and hell, progressive Jews and Christians entertain the possibility of universal salvation, the healing of all things, as well the reincarnation of the spirit from life to life. The image of universal salvation allows the possibility for each person to find her or his wholeness, while yet facing their imperfections, missed opportunities, and failures to love. From this perspective, God's love for us does not end at the grave, but continues to support and guide our future growth in a realm beyond earthly life. In this divine realm, there are no environmental impediments to our spiritual fulfillment. We will discover who we truly are in a community of love and adventure.

***Re-imaging reincarnation.*** Today, reincarnation—or a vision that joins reincarnation and reformed images of heaven—is a theological option for many progressive Jews and Christians. With the growing global spirituality and the influence of the New Age movement, reincarnation has become mainstream in certain segments of American society. At wedding receptions, book groups, and even temples and churches, persons talk about their "karma;" joke about who they were in a past life; or ponder their own personal evolution from life to life. To many persons, reincarnation provides great spiritual comfort. It affirms a continuity from life to life. We know that the next life will be similar to the past, with few surprises other than our name, family, and body. We do not need to worry about hell or eternal punishment, since eventually all persons will become enlightened and, according to the "rules" of reincarnation, the punishment for finite sins or imperfections is never extreme or arbitrary, but always fitting to the crime.

While reincarnation has made only a slight impact in mainstream Christianity and Judaism, still the image of evolution from life to life challenges Christians as well as Jews to rethink traditional images of the afterlife. To the surprise of many Jews in the twentieth and twenty-first centuries, the notion of a journey from life to life flows through the mystical Judaism of the Kabbalah. Certain contemporary Christians also suggest that reincarnation is a creative option to seeing our births as purely accidental or the result of God's arbitrary will.[5]

The Zohar, the classic text of thirteenth century Jewish mysticism, sees humankind journeying from life to life in search of its primordial unity with the Divine. While once the sparks of Divinity were united with their Creator in a lively flame of love, now they are dispersed throughout the universe, having forgotten their unity with God. Alienated from their Source, they plunge themselves into the maelstrom of violence, fear, anxiety, and competition. The beauty of the universe and physical embodiment is tainted—and often manipulated and abused—by their tunnel vision. As they look at the surface of life, these lost souls see only the boulder and not the angel within themselves and others poised to leap forth with the first glimmering of self-awareness. Nevertheless, according to the Zohar, God has not forsaken these souls. The Eternal has provided the mechanism of death and rebirth as the way to draw each soul closer to its true identity. The movement from life to life is the arena of growth, transformation, and eventual union with the Divine. The generosity of the Creator enables us to discover our true identities, give and receive forgiveness, and learn to love our neighbors and the Giver of Life with joyful intimacy.[6]

Whether our vision of survival after death embraces everlasting spiritual evolution in companionship with God or progressive growth toward the realization of Divine identity through the process of reincarnation, our postmortem adventures involve growing self-awareness, spiritual stature, and love. Consistent with today's near death experiences, Jewish mystics affirm that the first step in our spiritual journey beyond the grave is the life review. Each person experiences an instantaneous, colorful, and panoramic view of her or his lifetime at the moment of death. All the details of one's life are revealed in the blink of an eye. We come to understand the ecology of our lives and the impact of our actions on others. We discover firsthand the radical interdependence of life in the context of God's graceful love. In the words of Rabbi Eleazer,

> On the day when a person's time comes to depart from the world...three Messengers [the Angel of Love, who records a person's merits; the Angel of Judgment, who records our imperfections and missed opportunities; and the Angel of Mercy, who notes the length of a person's life] stand over her or him and take account of her or his life and all that he or she has done in the world. (Zohar I, 78b–79a)

In the eternal journey that joins the personal and cosmic adventures, none of our deeds is lost or forgotten. They live evermore in the mind of God. In similar fashion, Raymond Moody notes the graceful encounter with the Being of Light, who asks each person, "What have you to show me that you've done with your life?" As the Being of Light reveals our lives to us like snapshots in a photo album, the Divine makes comments that reveal the true nature of our encounters. In reflection on her near-death experience, one woman noted, "all through this, the Being kept stressing the importance of love."[7]

Jewish mystics note that in the three to seven days following death, the soul slowly disengages itself from the body. Like an old garment, the body must be discarded in order to prepare for the next stage of spiritual evolution, Purgatory. Similar to the traditional Roman Catholic notion of Purgatory, the Jewish mystics see this process of detachment as a time of refining, purifying, and transformation. During this time of spiritual engagement, the prayers and thoughts of the living may support the spirit's journey to its next adventure.

After everything that prevented the soul from experiencing its essential identity as a reflection of Divinity is spiritually cleansed, the soul enters Paradise, according to the Jewish mystics, where the soul further develops the emotional, spiritual, and intellectual qualities that are congruent with its previous lifetime. In Paradise, the soul experiences the ecstasy of inner peace and spiritual fulfillment as well as companionship with God.

However, according to the Kabbalah, the journey is not finished in Paradise. There is more to be learned in both the physical and spiritual realms. In the next stage of its journey, the soul returns to its Divine origin, where it prepares for its next incarnation in the world of the flesh. In the spirit of shalom, this place of preparation is a lively community of souls in which the radiant light of each soul's deepest identity warms its partners in their spiritual journey.

According to the Jewish mystics, the soul forgets this postmortem journey with its birth into a new body. Our spiritual amnesia is, surprisingly, a blessing in disguise—it enables us to claim our role in this lifetime, living in the here and now, rather than dwelling on the events of a past life. God knows that for mortals, one life at a time is more than enough! What the soul retains in this lifetime are those enduring lessons and truths that will shape its physical, emotional, intellectual, and spiritual evolution in its present incarnation. According to the mystical vision of reincarnation, we continue to experience the process of death and rebirth until we achieve spiritual unity with God. When we truly discover our Divine spark, the angel in the boulder of ignorance, suffering, and mortality, we are ready to claim fully our origin and destiny as God's beloved children. Like prisms, we will continue to reflect the light of our primordial creation as unique beings, but the light we will reflect is God's light shining through us without obstruction. Our light joins other enlightened souls to create a rainbow of love and beauty.

While progressive Christianity has given little attention to reincarnation, it affirms that our postmortem existence involves

Divine guidance and holy companionship with others. The afterlife is characterized by community, evolution, partnership, and spiritual growth. Christ, the Being of Light, guides us through an adventure of love, forgiveness, reconciliation, and healing that embraces all creation. Beyond the grave, by whatever processes God employs, our identity is refined and transformed so that we can become our fullest selves as God's children, joining all creation in a "heavenly" realm of love and creativity.

In contrast to religious conservatives and traditionalists who assert that our destiny is fixed at death, progressive Jews and Christians affirm that God's attitude toward us does not change at the moment of death; the God whose love guided our growth in the womb will guide us beyond the grave. Hell is not an option for the Loving God! While we are always free to choose against God, the Loving One will never choose against us! In the long run, God will heal the universe and every creature in it.

Progressive Christianity and Judaism provide a creative alternative to world-denying, individualistic, and punitive images of the afterlife. Our personal growth is always communal in nature. Our spiritual evolution contributes to the well-being of all creation and supports God's healing of the universe. What happens in this lifetime is important—justice here promotes evolution beyond the grave. The holistic vision of reality, characteristic of progressive Judaism and Christianity, goes beyond the dualism of this life and the next. We live one life in partnership with God's Holy Adventure and all creation, whether it be on this plane or another. Our economic, social, and ethical commitments in this life condition our neighbor's future lives as well as our own spiritual growth. We create our destiny in the afterlife by what we do today to bring wholeness and beauty to our world and to each human we encounter day-by-day.

While we can never fully fathom the afterlife, progressive Judaism and Christianity provide hope and courage to face the challenges of life even as we look toward eternity. We can face disability and death, knowing that we are in God's loving hands forever. The Eternal is always on our side and will provide everything we need to face our personal, relational, and planetary futures. Even as we embrace our mortality, we can trust God's faithful care. With spiritual pilgrims throughout the ages, we can proclaim nothing "will be able to separate us from the love of God" (Rom. 8:31–39). God will bring forth angels from all the boulders of life.

# CHAPTER THREE

# *Healing the Dying*

The philosopher Socrates once asserted that the lover of wisdom constantly prepares for her or his own death. Throughout the centuries, Buddhist and Christian monks have visited graveyards and meditated on skulls as a reminder of their mortality. Over 2500 years ago, the psalmist counseled his listeners that to gain a heart of wisdom, they needed to "count" their "days" and to recognize the brevity of life as well as God's eternity (Ps. 90:12).

The encounter with death can be the most significant catalyst to spiritual growth. Gautama Buddha's quest for enlightenment was inspired by his encounter, on successive days, with a dying man and a corpse. The young Indian prince realized that wealth and power could not immunize him from aging and death. Jesus' greatest triumph occurred when he followed the way of the cross rather than a life of comfort and safety. In Jesus' death, the surprising seeds of new life and healing were sown for his followers throughout the ages.

For our spiritual ancestors, the only path to healing went straight through the valley of the shadow of death. Though death surrounded them at every turn, the ancients wanted, above all, to have sufficient time to prepare for death by making peace with God and gathering their families around them for comfort and counsel.

Despite the radical changes in lifespan, medicine, and comfort care that the past two thousand years have brought to Western civilization, we are also aware of the brevity of life. When we least expect it, death may strike through a terrorist attack, an automobile accident, or a terminal illness.

Today, we need to create our own arts of dying. While we may not share the pre-scientific worldview of earlier generations or see humankind as suspended between heaven and hell, we still need practices that give us confidence and comfort in the face of death's inevitability. In order to move from denial to creative transformation, we need a vision of reality that gives us confidence in challenging times, spiritual practices that connect us with the Eternal in the midst of everyday life, and caring companionship at the edges of life.

In the previous chapter, we affirmed that the vision of a loving and eternal God and a creative and adventurous life beyond the grave provide confidence in the face of life's brevity. In this chapter, we will explore contemporary spiritual practices that enable us to face death while affirming the wonder and continuity of life. We will also suggest ways that we can experience life-affirming relationships in our living and dying.

The Jewish theologian Abraham Joshua Heschel asserted that the central question of the spiritual journey is not what we ask of God, but what God asks of us. Sickness, death, and bereavement, challenge us to the same fidelity, integrity, and love that is our calling in normal, everyday life. Even in our dying, we can be witnesses to the Divine Love that is our companion in every season of life. We can grow in virtue and spiritual stature even when we are facing death.

## Twenty-first Century Arts of Dying

How do we find hope and healing when death is a real possibility? How do we gain the spiritual stature to embrace death and yet affirm life? The ancient Christians invoked the term "martyr" to describe those who faced death by persecution with courage and fidelity to God. To be a martyr was to be a witness to God in challenging times. While we may never face religious persecution, our spiritual commitments can enable us to find courage and wholeness. We can be martyrs for God, individuals of spiritual stature, whose lives and deaths inspire others to find wholeness. Our living and dying can be our final gifts to God and our loved ones. In what Elisabeth Kübler-Ross calls "the final stage of growth," death can become a blessing to our world when we open ourselves to the wonders of this present moment and the spiritual resources hidden in every life situation. This task is challenging because it calls us to face our fears as well as our hopes without flinching. It calls us to become persons, whose spiritual stature embraces both light and darkness. Greatness of spirit, even at life's descending edges, arises from our commitment to practice our own version of the arts of dying by living according to certain life-supporting spiritual practices and affirmations. The following six spiritual affirmations enable us to experience wholeness in the midst of the dying process.

### *1. You Are More Than Your Fear and Pain*

The journey toward spiritual stature begins right where we are with the exploration of our current spiritual lives and attitudes toward death. Take a few minutes to be still and reflect on your own life. What painful issue or issues are dominating your attention? What fear or pain lurks beneath the surface or consciously threatens to undermine your well-being? Take a look at this fear or pain. Explore its many dimensions. See it for what it is in the context of the totality of your experience. Is this pain the *only* reality in your life and the only reality of your self? What positive realities still characterize your life? When pain threatens to constrict your self, imprisoning it in fearful isolation, take a moment to look beyond the present pain. See its relationship with your gifts, hopes and dreams; your loved ones and friends; your faith and relationship with God, the planet, and the cosmos. While recognizing the pain of your life, the struggles you face, and the reality of letting go of what once was normal, experience yourself as a person, whose stature and sense of relatedness are reflected in connectedness of your individual life with the whole of the cosmos.

Experience the spacious interconnectedness that gives birth to, and sustains, your life. In your original wholeness as a child of God, created in the Divine image, you are a person of stature and beauty. You are connected with infinite spiritual resources for the healing of body, mind, and spirit. In the midst of your pain and struggle, conclude with a prayer of gratitude for life's profound interdependence and the spiritual resources that lie within yourself, your relationships, and the Eternal One.

As they face life-threatening illness and the possibility of death, many persons experience this deep interconnectedness for the first time in their lives. Lifelong habits of individualism and fear of intimacy give way to profound experiences of interdependence and love.

The diagnosis of ALS (Lou Gehrig's Disease) obliterated Chip's carefully constructed world. Successful and independent, he believed he could make it on his own. Nevertheless, the prospect of disability and death undermined the foundations of Chip's self-sufficiency. He now had to depend on others for his care and support. For the first time in his life, this man, who always kept his feelings to himself, broke down in front of his wife. Throughout his life, Chip believed that if he shared his true feelings, people would ridicule him for his weakness. Worse than that, they might simply not respond to his feelings of pain. The child within him feared that if he started crying, he would never be able to stop, and that his fragile self would disintegrate. But as his wife cradled him that day with the same love that she had given their three children, Chip allowed himself to collapse, and in the process of breaking down, discovered that behind his shattered self lay the possibility of a richer and more powerful experience of life.

To his surprise, Chip discovered that his wife was really "there" for him. She heard his fears and dried his tears. She listened hour after hour to his concerns and in her listening, allowed an emerging new self to take shape.

As Chip's physical conditioned deteriorated, his wife and the visiting nurse bathed him and assisted him in going to the bathroom. In letting go of the illusion of independence, Chip discovered the courage, strength, and love that come from embracing a healthy interdependence. Chip experienced God's grace in the profound interconnectedness he found with his friends and family. Chip admits, "each day is painful. As I let go of one more thing that I once took for granted, sometimes I feel like giving up. But then I remember I am not alone in this journey. I have given up so much, but I have also gained so much. The love I've felt from my wife, family, and friends makes each day worth living and gives me hope to face the pain."

Though Chip's body has shrunk, his soul has grown in stature. Chip notes, "Before the illness, I felt it was me against the universe. Now, everything has changed. It hurts not to be able to go to the bathroom or move from place to place on my own. But now I have several hands to hold and several arms to lift me up. Now I feel as if God and the universe are with me in the loving touch and listening ears of my loved ones."

On his darkest days, Chips reminds himself of his true identity, "I have ALS, but I am more than my disease. As I look out my window, I am joined to the universe. As I touch my children or wife, I know that love is eternal. As I close my eyes, I feel God's nearness. I know that God is with me, but also within me—forever!"

We are more than our challenges. Our deepest selves are always connected with God. We have spiritual and relational resources that we cannot imagine. Practicing the art of creative connectedness and loving interdependence starts right now as we claim our larger self and reach out to God and our loved ones.

## 2. You Can Experience Peace through Practicing Forgiveness

On his deathbed, Rabbi Eleazer's students asked him for one last teaching. The dying rabbi responded, "you should repent one day before your death." His confused disciples asked him again, "How can we know just when that day comes?" To which Rabbi Eleazer replied, "You should repent every day."

In the ebb and flow of life, our imperfections and the imperfections of others confront us on a daily basis. Intentionally or unintentionally, we hurt our loved ones. We suffer slights, small and large, throughout the day. Sadly, many of us hold on both to our guilt and the shame and hurt we feel as a result of evils committed against us. The burden of emotional pain deadens our lives, destroys our relationships, and threatens to overwhelm us.

The reality of our imperfections becomes even more compelling as we face life's final journey. Some things we simply cannot undo. Those we have hurt may already have died or are alienated from us. Those who have hurt us may no longer be able to make amends. Out of self-protection, we may not wish to see persons whose actions have maimed our spirits and left a lifetime of pain. Still, our rebirth into the healing present challenges us to live by forgiveness.

Jesus once said to pray, "forgive us our debts, as we also have forgiven our debtors" (Mt. 6:12). Forgiveness is a dynamic process of letting go and making amends. During the Jewish days of awe and wonder, Rosh Hashanah and Yom Kippur, the primary spiritual act is *teschuvah* in Hebrew, or repentance. During this time, we confess our imperfection—our sins of commission and omission against the Divine, ourselves, and our neighbors. This confession prepares us to accept God's invitation to begin a new life of love and holiness.

Authentic wholeness in living and dying requires the interplay of confession and self-acceptance. The author of Psalm 139 proclaims:

> O [God], you have searched me and known me.
> You know when I sit down and when I rise up;
> > you discern my thoughts from far away.
> You search out my path and my lying down,
> > and are acquainted with all my ways.
> Even before a word is on my tongue,
> > O [Eternal One], you know it completely.
> You hem me in, behind and before,
> > and lay your hand upon me.
> Such knowledge is too wonderful for me;
> > it is so high that I cannot attain it. (Ps. 139:1–6)

We are known by God, and in being known by the Divine Lover we can embrace the totality of our own experience—our greatness and our weakness.

Today, researchers speak of the "forgiveness factor." Personal experience as well as scientific research suggests that forgiveness and unforgiveness may be factors in health and illness. Bearing the burden of guilt and unforgiveness diminishes our quality of life and threatens our relationships, and may eventually compromise our immune and cardiovascular systems. Without forgiveness, both Divine and human, the burdens of life become too great to bear.

There is no one behavior that will insure authentic forgiveness. In the spirit of Dietrich Bonhoeffer, the Lutheran pastor who was executed in a German concentration camp after being convicted for participating in an unsuccessful plot to kill Hitler, we believe that Divine forgiveness is free, but never cheap. Healthy forgiveness is not for the fainthearted, but requires us to face God, ourselves, and others just as we are without masks or illusions. It may require us to change our lives and face the impact of previous choices we have made.

Forgiveness is grounded in our vision of reality. We can seek, accept, and share forgiveness because of God's love for us. The One who knows us fully also loves us fully. Though our imperfections cause God pain, God works through our imperfections to bring us healing. At any moment in life, from birth to death, forgiveness is a possibility. Despite our turning from God, the Eternal One is always ready to welcome us home. Although we must face the consequences of our words and behaviors, God will heal our wounds and restore us to wholeness. God, however, still needs us to recognize our pain and the pain we have caused others in order to complete the circle of forgiveness. In the words of Psalm 51:

> Have mercy upon me, O God,
>> according to your steadfast love;
> according to your abundant mercy
>> blot out my transgressions.
> Wash me thoroughly from my iniquity,
>> and cleanse me from sin....
> Create in me a clean heart, O God,
>> and put a new and right spirit within me.
>> (Ps. 51:1, 2, 10)

A few hundred years later, Jesus told the story of a sinner who came to the Temple in Jerusalem, so filled with his unworthiness that he looked downward and cried out, "Lord, have mercy upon me, a sinner." In the Eastern Orthodox Christian tradition, this prayer evolved to become the "prayer of the heart" or "Jesus' prayer," a Christian mantra whose words are "Lord Jesus Christ, Son of God, have mercy upon me, a sinner." Short versions of this prayer simply cry out, "Have mercy" or "Christ have mercy," or "Lord, have mercy." Similar to Jewish practice of *teschuvah,* this prayer seeks the Divine mercy that enables us to overcome alienation and begin a new chapter in our personal pilgrimage.

To many moderns, the idea of sin is archaic and superstitious. Nevertheless, forgiveness in all its dimensions requires us to embrace our pain and regret, experience imaginatively the pain we have caused others, and then seek healing in relationship with God and others. We can experience Divine Love through both traditional and modern practices of forgiveness: the "examination of conscience" found in both the Jewish and Christian spiritual traditions; the death bed confessions of Judaism; and the "life reviews" of the near death experiences. This examination of conscience is the heart of Rabbi Eleazer's counsel to repent every day because no one knows her or his final hour.

## AN EXAMINATION OF CONSCIENCE

In daily examination of conscience, we take time at the end of each day to reflect briefly on the spiritual quality of the day. What was the quality of our interactions? Where did we experience pain or hurt? Where might we have hurt, intentionally or unintentionally, another person? What was our state of mind—calm, anxious, fearful, angry—throughout the day? What was the quality of our heart—open and loving, closed and alienated? What was the quality of our spiritual life and relationship with God? Were we attentive to God throughout the day or forgetful? Where did we experience God moments? Where did we live as if God were absent or nonexistent?

Following these moments of self-examination, we simply ask for God's mercy and God's grace to begin anew in the morning. We may choose to imagine God as our companion and place, one by one, our burdens of guilt and pain in God's hands, letting God carry the load, so that we can begin the new day with freshness. If we have hurt someone during the day, we may pray for guidance about how best to make amends and ask for forgiveness.

In preparation for seeking forgiveness and beginning anew in a relationship, review the situation, feeling the pain that has been caused. Invite God into the scene as the Lover of all the parties involved. Experience God joining you with the one you have hurt or the one who has hurt you. Experience imaginatively a moment of reconciliation—by word or deed. Ask God to show you what will bring healing to this particular situation. As you place you life in God's hands, you open the door to healing and love.

### DEATHBED CONFESSION

The *Viddui,* or death bed confession, enables the individual to make peace with God by recognizing her or his imperfections, expressing regret about missed opportunities and neglected possibilities, and acknowledging where he or she has not lived up to his or her divine potential. In sharing one's life in its fullness with God, a person experiences God's acceptance and forgiveness.

> I acknowledge unto You, O Eternal, my God and God of my ancestors, that both my cure and my life are in Your hands. May it be your will to send me a perfect healing. Yet, if death lies before me, I will accept it. I recognize my imperfection and failure to achieve my full potential as your creation. Grant me the abounding happiness that is treasured for your children. At this hour of death, make known to me the path of life: in your presence is the fullness of joy and bliss forever. You Who are the protector of the bereaved and the helpless, watch over my loved ones with whose soul my own is linked. Into your hand, I commit my spirit; redeem and transform it, O Eternal God of Truth.[1]

### HEALING THE PAST

Forgiveness frees us from the bondage of the past as it welcomes us to the spaciousness of God's Loving Present. At the heart of forgiveness is the healing of memories. While we cannot change the reality of the past, we can transform its meaning for us in the present and future.

In the healing of memories, we return to a past experience and invite God to be with us to soothe the pain, ask for forgiveness, or forgive another. Healing of memories is especially effective, when we can no longer address the person or persons involved directly.

Find a comfortable position, breathing gently and deeply into God's presence. Reflect on a past painful event, visualizing the scene, remembering the pain, recognizing the possibility that the event could have been very different. As you reflect on the painful event, whether you are seeking to forgive or be forgiven, invite the Divine to be your companion. See the other from the perspective of God's creative love. Experience her or his own pain and hurt. Experience God joining you and the one with whom you are alienated in a healing manner, perhaps, by surrounding you and the other, or others, in a circle of love and joining hands with each one present. Let go of the burden of hurt or guilt by placing it in God's hands. Ask God to help you say what needs to be said as you share your feelings and seek reconciliation. Experience God's light of forgiveness enveloping all persons concerned. Conclude with a prayer of thanksgiving for God's healing touch.

If you have hurt another person, with whom you still have the opportunity to communicate, make a sincere effort to ask for forgiveness and seek reconciliation, if it is appropriate for you to do so. As you reach out to the other, seeking reconciliation, know that God is present in your attempts at new life.

If the pain is so great that you cannot forgive the other, let go of any self-judgment as you place your unforgiveness and pain in God's loving arms. There are certain personal and political abuses and atrocities that we should never forget, and may never forgive. What we cannot forgive, because of its deep pain and destructive impact on our lives, we commit to God whose love seeks to heal our pain as well as the sins of the perpetrator or abuser. Even the smallest effort at spiritual reconciliation transforms ourselves and our relationships. Ultimately forgiveness is a graceful intent whose foundation is in God's love and not our own efforts.[2]

### A Spiritual Life Review

Self-forgiveness involves recognizing both our goodness and imperfection. In the spirit of the "life review" reported by persons who have had near death experiences, this exercise invites you imaginatively to encounter the Being of Light.

In a relaxed and comfortable position, take time to breathe in Divine peace and protection. Imagine that this is the last day of your life. You are taking a journey down a long tunnel from life to death. You encounter a Luminous Being. What does this being look like? Do you identify it with any particular religious personage? As you encounter this Being of Light, you feel yourself embraced by loving arms and graceful acceptance.

In this place of comfort and safety, the Being of Light invites you to look at your life, as it asks you certain questions:

What was the high point of your life?
When were you happiest?
Did you fulfill your dreams?
What opportunities did you miss?
What were your successes and failures?
What are you most thankful for in your life?
What opportunities for love did you embrace? Which ones passed you by?
When did you feel most alive?
When did God seem most real?
Where do you need to go with your life, when you return to everyday life?

Let each question invite you to both reflection and imagination. Like Ebenezer Scrooge, you can confront the ghosts of the past with the hope that your life may be transformed through forgiveness and love.

### 3. You Can Experience Eternity Every Day

The reports of near death experiences inspire us, in part, because they remind us that we don't have to wait for the afterlife to experience love and beauty. God's eternity permeates this world. Though it often seems hidden, God's holy adventure is right here and now. We don't have to die to experience God's dream for our lives.

We prepare for dying simply by living with awareness of the unrepeatable beauty and wonder of each moment. Even in its challenges, each new day is an opportunity to live in companionship with the Holy Adventure.

What would your life be like, if you really believed that today was God's holy day and that each moment springs from eternity? In *Tuesdays with Morrie,* Mitch Albom asks his college professor and spiritual mentor Morrie Schwartz to imagine his perfect day. Bedridden and anticipating his own death, Morrie surprises Mitch with his response:

> I'd get up in the morning, do my exercises, have a lovely breakfast of sweet rolls and tea, go for a swim, and then have my friends over for a nice lunch. I'd have them come over one or two at a time, so that we could talk about their families, their issues, about how much we mean to each other. Then I'd go for a walk, in a garden with some trees, watch their colors, watch the birds, take in the nature that I haven't seen in so long now. In the evening, we'd all go to a restaurant with some great pasta, maybe some duck, I love duck, and then we'd dance the rest of the night. I'd dance with all the wonderful partners out there, until I was exhausted. And then I'd go home and have a deep, wonderful sleep.[3]

Our willingness to live in the present moment without regret or denial can awaken us to eternal life in the midst of everyday toils of medication, IV's, disability, and impending death. Two days before her death, Beth's mother, who was dying from cardiovascular disease, shared her inner peace with her daughter. "I'm ready to go. I'd like to have more time, but I know it's time." Beth asked her mother, "If you had more time, and were healthy, what would you do with your life?" Her mother's response was clear and honest, "I would be more kind and loving." Her counsel speaks to us today. We are building our eternity every moment. Every encounter gives us the opportunity to choose life and to expand the beauty of the universe. We can be more loving right here and now!

In the pure simplicity of embracing each moment as holy, we discover the Eternal Now. We can see God's face in the care of the physicians and nurses. God's touch comes to us in the caress of a spouse or friend. The Divine voice echoes through every "I love you."

### LIVING A PERFECT DAY

Imaging your perfect day can inspire you to live each day in the presence of God's shalom. As you begin this exercise, simply be still, letting your mind rest in the fullness of life and the goodness of God. Imagine yourself awakening to your perfect day, the day in which beauty and love shape your concrete reality. Follow yourself throughout the day. How does your day begin? What activities shape your day? What would you like to eat? Who would you like to see? What would you like to say to your companions? What acts of kindness would you like to share? What spiritual experiences would bring unity and wholeness to your day?

As the day draws toward an end, for what things are you are you most thankful? What are your hopes for the day ahead? With whom would you like to spend the last waking moments of the day? What words would conclude your day?

As you enjoy your image of a perfect day, ponder ways that you can embody this day in your normal life. While we can seldom achieve all our dreams in any particular day, we can experience beauty, rest, love, and adventure in each new day.

Following this meditation, take a moment to jot down or journal the actions that you *can* bring to your next day, and those you can incorporate in the days ahead. In the weeks to come, keep track of your ability to live out your "perfect day." Even persons who are seriously ill can integrate moments of joy, wonder, love, creativity, and adventure in their days.

Imagining our perfect day reminds us that each day is a call for radical amazement. As Ram Dass notes, following a stroke that led to partial paralysis, "I'm still here," and that simple reality is always a blessing. As the prophet affirms, God's mercies are new every morning, unfolding in surprising ways each second of the day.

## 4. Experience Gratitude in Every Life Situation

Life can be difficult. Pain and injustice abound in our individual and communal lives. But within each moment Divine beauty can spring forth and change everything. Speaking out of his own experiences of imprisonment and physical disability, the early Christian teacher Paul proclaims:

> Rejoice in the Lord always; again, I will say, Rejoice. Let your gentleness be known to everyone. The Lord is near. Do not worry about anything, but in everything by prayer and supplication with thanksgiving let your requests be made known to God. And the peace of God, which surpasses all understanding, will guard your hearts and minds in Christ Jesus. (Phil. 4:4–7)

Despite their Christian origins, these words have a universal meaning. Even in tragedy, struggle, sickness, and death, we can experience joy because of God's ever-present care. God is faithful in every season of life. God provides for our deepest needs. But we need to open our eyes to the abundance that surrounds us.

Gratitude awakens us to the bounty of Divine and human support. No stranger to the suffering and injustice of life, Abraham Joshua Heschel affirmed:

Just to be is a blessing.
Just to live is holy.

Radical amazement and gratitude are one in the same. Pain and fear constrict, while gratitude awakens us to God's constant and subtle presence in our lives. Praise and thanksgiving are among the greatest spiritual virtues.

Aware of the life's awesome wonder, we share in the great "yes" of Divine creativity and faithfulness. Traditional Jewish and Christian funeral services focus on God's faithfulness and love, first and foremost. Though we may eulogize the deceased, we gather primarily at funerals to affirm God's never-ending fidelity and care, which embraces both life and death. We gather, in all our grief and pain, to say "yes" and "thank you" for what has been, and affirm our trusting openness in what will be.

### WALKING IN GRATITUDE

We can experience God's blessings in tragedy as well as joy. In that spirit, we invite you to go on a "gratitude walk." Whether your pace is slow or aerobic in cadence, take some time simply to look around you as you walk. Experience the wonder of movement, of the senses, of the ambient earth. Bathe your senses in the form and color of plants and trees, the harmony of human and nonhuman sound, the extravagance of human creativity (if you are walking in the city). Ponder life's gifts to you. As you recount each one, you may choose to affirm your gratitude to God and others, "I thank you for _____." Let words of thanks pour forth from your heart and mind. What you will discover, whether your walk is just around the block or over a mountain, is that it is virtually impossible to run out of things for which to be thankful in your relationships, in the beauty of nature, and in your own giftedness and uniqueness.

If your physical condition makes walking difficult or impossible, simply relax in your bed, imaging yourself on a pilgrimage through life in which you notice all the blessings you have received. Take time on this imaginative journey to stop and experience the joy of life's wonder. Recall positive experiences and moments of healing and love. Visualize those persons who have been most pivotal in your life adventure.

Filled with the spirit of gratitude, commit yourself to words of thanksgiving in every positive encounter—a note or e-mail from a friend, physician's phone call, a nurse's or orderly's support, a desk clerk's directions to your appointment, a spouse or friend's company at a medical test. You will discover something utterly amazing—the essential blessedness and giftedness of life and the abundant hand of its Giver. Like young Annie Dillard, who grew up to become one of America's most creative writers, you will experience the world as a place in which God's magic pennies are abundantly strewn in every direction, just waiting to be discovered by each passerby.

### 5. You Can Be Generous in Every Life Situation

The Jewish and Christian sages proclaim the unity of receiving and giving. Because God's generosity has given us life, we share generously with others. The open system of Divine Creativity is not governed by the principles of "zero-sum" or "bottom line" economics. The evolving world is ever-abundant and creative. The more we give, the more we receive. The more we love, the more we are able to love. The more we create, the more effortless creativity becomes for us. In the spirit of Jesus' image, God is the vine and we are the branches. Divine energy is constantly flowing through us. We just need to open the door to this creative and life-supporting fullness.

In the ancient world, making a will involved much more than the dispersing of assets. When a person shared their last will and testament with loved ones or political successors, they passed on their values and wisdom to the next generation. Their words lived on immortally in the values and actions of their children and grandchildren.

While we encourage you to plan for the responsible allocation of your financial resources to your family and charities (after all, one of us is a professor of tax law!), we invite you to ponder another kind of will—a truly "living will." This will embraces not only your "advance directives" for medical care and your health care power of attorney, but also the values you want to pass on to your family members and friends. Your "last words," whether written or spoken, can change someone's life forever.

### MAKING YOUR LIVING WILL

Take some time to relax in the abundance of life. Ask for Divine guidance in your meditation. Reflect upon the lessons you have learned, the gifts you have received, and the wisdom that has shaped your life. Looking at your life and relationships, which persons would benefit most from your wisdom and life experience? In what ways, can you best share these gifts of wisdom—spoken word, a note, a personal creed, an audio or video tape or CD, a painting or photograph? If you were to die tomorrow, what blessing would you give to those nearest you?

Whether you are in the process of dying or envisage many years ahead of you, begin to plan ways you can share the wisdom you have gained from your life journey. Remember the interplay of form and content, of giving and receiving. Listen to the other person well enough so that your words truly speak to her or his heart. Be willing to let the other be your teacher as well, whether she or he is five or ninety five years old. Our generosity opens the channels of giving and receiving in companionship with the Generous Source of all good gifts.

## 6. You Can Walk in the Light

*With God as my companion, today can be a good day to die and to live! Even in life's struggles, I walk in the light.* Native American warriors prepared for battle with the affirmation, "Today is a good day to die." Recognizing the potential for cowardice, they reminded themselves of the deeper heroism that would sustain them in the conflict.

As we face our deaths, God calls us to be partners in an heroic adventure. The path ahead is unfamiliar, but God will lead us one step at a time and the Holy One will give us the spiritual, emotional, and relational resources to be victorious even when the physical battle is lost. Facing his own death as a witness for Jesus of Nazareth and the God of Israel, the apostle Paul proclaimed, "in all things, we are more than conquerors," because nothing "will be able to separate us from the love of God" (Rom. 8:37–39). Centuries before, a Jewish spiritual leader affirmed that "[God] is my light and my salvation; whom shall I fear?" (Ps. 27:1).

There is no reason to romanticize the dying process. Death in our technological age is often painful, lonely, and dehumanizing. Facing the pain and darkness that may lie ahead requires all the courage we can muster. Walking through the valley of the shadow of death challenges us to trust the adventure that lies ahead and the Adventurer who walks beside us. With every breath and thought, we can affirm that God is our light and our salvation, and that God's light is stronger than any darkness we experience.

### WALKING WITH GOD

Whether sitting or lying down, take time to breathe slowly and intentionally. As you close your eyes, reflect on your current life situation—feelings of pain, helplessness, fear, hope, and expectation. Imagine that you are not alone with these many feelings. Visualize the Holy One—in whatever way seems appropriate—as your companion, taking your hand along the pathway. Feel the Divine guiding you through the rough spots and comforting you in your pain and suffering.

Ahead on the path lies a final bend that leads to death itself. Step by step, walk toward that ultimate destination. As you come to death's doorway, God is with you. God takes your hand and leads you to the other side. With God as your companion, what surprises or wonders do you discover on the other side? As you journey into the afterlife, God will be with you every step of the way.

## BREATHING GOD'S LIGHT

Often during the final days of their lives, many persons are counseled to go toward the light. In reality, there is a no spiritual reason to "go" toward the light, because the light is always here with us. In this meditation, we simply invite persons who are in the process of dying and their companions to become aware of the Divine Light that is within and around them by gently breathing its radiance.

In the quiet, inhale the light of God, allowing it to permeate every cell of your body and enabling it to calm and cleanse your mind. Experience yourself as filled with light and surrounded by that same healing light. Feel the Divine Light bringing you a sense of pace and well being, regardless of your current health condition. You are a spark of Divinity, always dwelling in God's light. In this moment, let yourself experience your deepest reality. Let the light shine in and through you, so that you can journey forth as a bearer of the Light. With God as your companion, there is always something more!

## AFFIRMATIONS AT LIFE'S DESCENDING EDGES

In a society that vacillates between the denial of death and the aggressive battle against death, we need positive affirmations and images of death and dying. While we encourage you to create your own healing affirmations, the following affirmations may be helpful in nurturing spiritual transformation in difficult times.

I am in God's hands regardless of what the future brings.

My spirit is eternal and creative.

God is my companion in life and death.

God's light guides me into eternity.

Love is stronger than death.

I can love and receive love regardless of my health condition.

In life and death, I am surrounded by Divine Light.

I am an eternal child of God.

The following affirmations may be helpful in transforming your attitudes toward persons who are dying.

My _____ is in God's hands.

I can communicate my love to _____ regardless of her or his health condition.

Nothing can separate us from God's love.

I have all the love and energy to respond creatively to

_____.

I let go of grievances toward _____ and live by God's love.

I give and receive love in my relationship with

_____.

## Caring for the Dying and Caring for Ourselves

We exist in a lively and intricate web of relationships in which our well-being is connected with health and wholeness of others. No one lives or dies alone, but in a community of relationships which either nurtures or hinders their growth. Recognition of this profound interconnectedness is essential if we are to be healthy caregivers for loved ones at life's edges.

*You can care for yourself while you care for others.* A plaque at the College of Surgeons in Paris notes, "we are the dying caring for the dying." This reality is both sobering and empowering. Nowhere is our solidarity with the dying more obvious than in caring for loved ones during their dying process. In the care of a child of a parent, a parent of a child, or one spouse of another, we learn that love is stronger than death. In caring for the vulnerable, we discover that the meaning of marriage vows goes far beyond husband and wife, but embraces any committed long term relationship—"for better, for worse;

for richer, for poorer; in sickness and in health; to love and to cherish until death do us part." Yet too often the needs of the caregiver are overlooked or put aside in order to care for a child, parent, or spouse who is dying. The pain, suffering, and fatigue of caregivers is often forgotten by their churches and temples, and even the caregivers themselves who feel that they must soldier on, regardless of the cost to themselves or their other significant relationships. While it is obvious that the care and comfort of dying in their final days is a moral and spiritual imperative, our ability to sacrifice for their needs in a healthy way depends on our willingness to care for ourselves as well.

To the surprise of many first-time air passengers, at the beginning of every flight, the airline attendant announces, "in case of a loss of cabin pressure, put on your oxygen mask first. Then, place a mask on your child or dependent." The wisdom behind this comment is that if we lose consciousness and cannot take of ourselves, we will not be able to care for those who depend upon us.

In the dynamic web of life, giving and receiving constitute one dynamic reality. We are challenged to love our neighbors, but also to love ourselves, in order to realize our potential in the divine-human relationship. Accordingly, if you truly want to be helpful to a dying friend or relative, you need to commit yourself to your own wholeness through the regular practices of prayer, meditation, love, forgiveness, and honest communication. The consequences of neglecting your own self-care are often experienced as fatigue, stress, burn out, anger and abusive comments, and physical and mental illness.

We need always to remember that the dying are still living! However, just as importantly, we also need to remember that their caregivers still have a life outside the hospital room or the daily care and comfort of loved ones at home. An intricate ecology joins dying persons and their caregivers in the quest for wholeness. Despite their different circumstances, what heals the dying also brings wholeness to the caregiver. In terms of relationships, this means that companionship, acceptance, affirmation, healthy touch, comfort, rest, and a sense of community are essential to the spiritual and physical well-being of persons facing terminal illness as well as their caregivers.

Dying persons need to know that we will not abandon them. They need to know that we will give them high touch through words and hands in the midst of the high tech world of Western medicine. They need to know that their lives are not encompassed by their physical condition, life expectancy, or hospital room.

Caregivers also need to know that they have a personal life beyond their responsibility to care and comfort. Caregivers need to know that they are not alone and that they have the communal resources to face the final journey with someone they love. Caregivers need high touch even as they respond to the spiritual needs of a child, spouse, or a parent. They need a world beyond the daily duties of loving care.

The African proverb notes, "it takes a village to raise a child." It also takes a village to care for a dying friend or relative. The vision of shalom that inspires both Judaism and Christianity challenges us to create communities of care. In the interdependence of life, the well-being of one contributes to the well being of others. We can support caregivers, first, by our simple awareness that they cannot go it alone!

If you are unsure about what would be helpful to a caregiving friend or acquaintance, we suggest that you follow two basic spiritual principles—*imagination* and *listening.*

### An Exercise in Caring Imagination

Take a few unhurried moments to look at your own life. Who depends on you? Who needs your care? Toward whom do you feel certain unique obligations? Visualize your loved ones and dependants.

If this person were dying or seriously disabled, what would you need to do to respond to their needs? In what ways would it change your life? What stresses would it add to your life? Experience how a day of constant care would change your life.

If you found yourself as a loving caregiver, whom could you count on to respond to your needs? Visualize those upon whom you can depend in difficult times.

When Bruce's father was placed in a nursing home following a paralyzing stroke, Bruce experienced the kindness and commitment of his father's church community. Three thousand miles from his father and disabled brother, Bruce could not personally provide hands on care. For the five years Bruce's father lived in a nursing home, an informal group of senior adults (the "young guys" in their 70s and 80s) regularly visited Bruce's father. They took him communion, addressed issues of care with the nursing home staff, and invited Bruce's brother out to eat on a weekly basis. While none of these men thought they were doing anything extraordinary, their care was a holy work done in response to God's lovingkindness. They responded to Bruce's dad, as if he were Christ, "in the least of these."

### Listening with Love

Dying persons and their caregivers need our silence as well as our words. Too often, we fill the empty spaces with words. We fear the apparent helplessness of silence. We have heard the maxim, "don't stand there, do something" and so we problem solve without discovering the deepest needs of the other.

Theologian Nelle Morton notes that we "listen each other into speech." With our silence or with simple questions, we allow the other—the dying person or her or his caregiver—to share her or his life with us. When we hear both their spoken and unspoken life story, we can respond lovingly and creatively in terms of what they really need from us.

In our experience, caregivers often need the basics of normal life to get them through the challenge of loving companionship with a dying relative or friend. Caregivers need "Sabbath time"—that is, time to rest, sleep in, meditate, and go to church or temple. Caregivers also need time for physical and emotional re-creation and renewal—a visit to the beauty salon, a walk in the woods, a movie or play, a leisurely trip to the mall or shopping center. Caregivers need companionship—someone to listen, to affirm, and to hug; someone with whom they can be honest with their pain, frustration, and fear. Caregivers need spiritual nurture—someone with whom to pray as well as to be silent.

### Knowing Your Limits

We are neither omnipotent nor impotent. We can't do everything, nor are we passive spectators in life's adventures. The challenge for caregivers is to know our limits and to know when to let go of the ideal in order to bring wholeness to the real world in which we live.

After his father's stroke, Bruce's family did everything it could to enable his father, Everett, to move back home. They encouraged him to commit himself to rehabilitation—to strengthen his arms and legs, and to learn to use his muscles in new ways. They contemplated hiring a home care aide and remodeling the house. Nevertheless, after weeks of reflection, they made the hard decision of moving Bruce's father into a nursing home. Their private geriatric social worker, Sally Hedman, told the family bluntly one afternoon, "Everett can't return home. Your handicapped brother can't give him the care he needs, and Bruce, you can't supervise the home care staff from 3000 miles away."

Bruce and his family felt both guilt and sadness. They felt they had let Everett down. The family, however, could still do something. While Everett was still in rehabilitation, Bruce explored nursing homes throughout the Santa Clara Valley in California and found a small, family-owned nursing home, just two miles from the home where Bruce's father and handicapped brother had lived. Synchronously, Bruce's father, a retired minister, had visited persons in the home over a thirty-year period. Although Bruce's family had limits in time, money, and energy, still they found the right home for Bruce's father, and this place was a blessing to Everett and Bill, Bruce's brother.

Hard decisions need to be made at times. Faced with their limits, caregivers must tearfully call in professional caregivers, move parents to assisted living or nursing home environments, or exercise their responsibility as medical power of attorney to determine the most appropriate health care. Even though it may be the best thing to do, few children feel comfortable telling the physician, "let my parent die." Thanks to the hospice movement, dying persons and their families receive guidance, spiritual support, and practical care throughout the dying process. This enables them to respond creatively to their feelings of guilt, impotence, and grief at the death of a loved one.

In the ecology of life, we are created for caring. We find our greatest joy in returning the love that we have received and bringing beauty to those in need. However, our greatest gifts burst forth when our care embraces our own lives as our offering to God and those in need.

## Your Love Can Bring Healing to Dying Persons

In the biblical tradition, love is a verb. Inspired by God's love for us, we channel Divine love to others. In our interpersonal relationships, we hear the Divine question and receive the Divine imperative. Do you love your neighbor? Do you care for the lonely and vulnerable? Do you respond to the cries of the human heart?

Echoing the voice of God, the prophet asks, "what does [God] require of you?" and receives the Divine challenge, "to do justice, and to love kindness, and to walk humbly with your God" (Mic. 6:8). At the last judgment, the Divine "life review," the righteous and unrighteous ask, "When did we see you, Lord?" The Divine One responds:

I was hungry and you gave me food, I was thirsty and you gave me something to drink, I was a stranger and you welcomed me, I was naked and you gave me clothing, I was sick and you took care of me, I was in prison and you visited me....just as you did to one of the least of these who are members of my family, you did it to me" (Mt. 25:35–36, 40).

We are all members of the Divine family. Our own healing and wholeness depends on our care for others, especially the vulnerable, lonely, lost, and dying. Our ability to become "healing partners" with persons who are dying is grounded first in imagination and vision. Jesus told his disciples to look for the Divine in persons at the margins of society and everyday life. Kabbalistic mysticism challenges us to see holiness within each human being. In seeing the hidden angel within each boulder, we enable the sick and dying, the helpless and lonely, to experience their true destiny as God's children.

Neither Jesus nor the Jewish mystics had any illusions about the ease of seeing the other's hidden holiness. Our "angelic" identity can be hidden by anger at helplessness, by depression at impending death, and by alienation at relatives and friends who neither call nor visit. Tubes and medication can dim our perception of the spiritual essence of a person. Confusion, dementia, and pharmaceutically-induced irrationality, can make conversations and encounters awkward. Yet beneath the painful exterior, the light of God is undimmed. The boulders are real and can never be denied. Nevertheless, loving care finds an angel in life's most jagged edges. We can liberate the angel within through caring companionship, comfort and touch, listening and receiving, nurturing the spirit, and connecting in community.

### You Can Be a Caring Companion

Each time she left her mother at the nursing home, Susan's heart broke as she heard the words, "please don't leave me alone. I'm afraid." Susan knew she could not stay forever, but her mother's words pierced her soul. Susan had a husband and three small children. The hours she spent at the nursing home with her dying mother were the center around which she planned each day. "Mom gave me so much when I was a child.

I'm just giving back." Still, she could not be with her mother twenty-four hours a day. Susan had to trust the staff of the nursing home and the hospice team as well as her mother's inner resources each time she left the facility.

Throughout our life journey, we need the comfort of loving arms. Sickness brings forth feelings of dependence and vulnerability. We need to know that someone cares enough to be our companion in life and death. Facing our own limits and mortality enables us to be present for those whose dying is imminent. We need the real presence of another human being, who becomes the embodied presence of God for us.

At the heart of the Jewish and Christian traditions is the affirmation that although the God of the universe is always with us, God also sends persons into our lives who share God's love and wisdom in tangible, embodied ways. Each one of us can identify God's messengers in our lives. Still we are called to share what we have received with others. By our faithfulness, we may become the incarnation of God for chronically ill and dying persons just as Jesus, Christians believe, revealed in human flesh the loving heart of God.

### You Can Comfort and Touch

Few persons die without some degree of pain and indignity. Many of today's most effective medical advances leave persons feeling alone, manipulated, and dehumanized. In her account of her mother's dying, *A Very Easy Death,* Simone de Beauvoir recoils at the dehumanization of technological medicine with the cry, "please don't leave her in the power of the brutes."[4]

Today, hospices have coined the term "comfort care." When death is likely, issues of presence, comfort, and spiritual growth come to the forefront. As life ebbs, it is imperative that pain be kept at a minimum. Unremitting and severe pain shrinks our world to our present suffering and our fear of more suffering to come. We are unable, if the pain is too great, to reach out to others in love, to say our "good-byes," or to address the deeper spiritual issues of life. If possible, patients themselves should have a role in determining the amount of pain medication they receive. Control of pain medication serves both to relieve pain as it arises as well as to preserve the patient's dignity and self-determination. The goal of supportive medication is to balance pain relief with the promotion of conscious awareness as much as possible. As hospice chaplain Jeanne Brenneis notes, "when physical pain is minimized, persons can address the deeper pain of life—leaving their friends and family—as well as their relationship with God."

When caring companions are present, patients do not have to wait to go to the bathroom or sit forlornly for tests or chemotherapy treatments. If a community of caregivers is gathered, patients need not face the darkness of sleepless nights alone. Someone beside them represents the Divine Love that gently and anonymously surrounds all of us.

Touch can be healing at any stage of life. When his father was dying, Michael crawled into bed with him, spooning and embracing his father's shrunken body, reading Psalms and stories from the Hasidic tradition to his Orthodox Jewish father. Bruce and his wife Kate regularly give Reiki healing touch treatments to persons following chemotherapy or in their hospital beds. They believe that Reiki healing touch mediates and focuses Divine healing energy to bring balance and healing to mind, body, and spirit. Touch connects us with the universe and reminds us that we are worth touching—that our bodies still matter and that we belong to the human community. Gentle physical touch permeates one's whole being and caresses the spirit.

### Listening into Love

We hear each other into life and love. Often the dying need our presence more than our words. A habit of simple listening—to labored breath, fears and concerns, hopes and dreams—creates a spacious environment in which surprising graces can be experienced. Authentic listening enables the dying person to share her or his heart. Dying persons do not need "baby talk" or to be treated as if they are children. In listening and asking meaningful questions, we affirm their value and their ability to share their gifts. If receiving is an essential element in loving relationships, then listening is one of its prerequisites. In the company of the dying and sick, we often feel awkward and worried that we will say the wrong thing. Surprisingly, instead of observing spiritual silence, we often babble incessantly when we have nothing to say. We are tuned in to transmission, when we should be receiving. In listening, we let the other person shape our lives and reveal God's presence to us.

Following her father's death, Wendy realized that their most significant bonding occurred in moments of quiet contemplation as the two of them gazed out the bedroom window at the butterflies in her parents' garden. Every now and then, her father would share a story from his youth or a funny experience from her childhood. He would share his worries about her mother's life after he was gone. Toward the end of her father's life, Wendy was astounded when this rational engineer began to speak about seeing angels and divine messengers. Wendy admits in retrospect that listening became a spiritual discipline for her. Usually extroverted and talkative, Wendy challenged herself to wait on her father, to avoid completing his sentences, and to ask questions rather than give answers. "It was wonderful simply to be with the man whose love had shaped my own life. I felt I was on holy ground and that in the distance I could hear the sound of angels' wings flapping."

Listening was at the heart of Jesus' ministry. In his encounters with the sick, Jesus often asked open-ended questions, such as: "Do you want to be healed?" or "What do you want me to do for you?" In asking questions, we may discover unexpected wonders in persons who had seemed one-dimensional to us before. One way to open up conversation with a dying elder is to ask them to reflect on important moments in their lives. This opens the door to generative sharing as well as thanksgiving for what has been. With certain people, we may feel comfortable asking about their feelings about their illness and impending death, or where God is in their lives. With more physically able and mentally alert persons, we may ask them to write a brief spiritual biography or account of what it was like to grow up on the farm, live through the Great Depression, attend Woodstock, or serve in Vietnam or World War II. We ask such questions in order to listen, learn, and let the Divine spark emerge from the other.

God is present and seeking beauty even when persons are comatose. While we may not choose ask to questions, we can hold their hand, caress their fingers, play their favorite music, and share our own visions of God with them. Even when consciousness fades, God's still, small voice echoes lovingly in the halls of the unconscious mind.

Listening lovingly opens the door for the generosity and the sharing of wisdom that promotes wholeness for the dying and their loved ones. As we listen, the dying person knows that we honor her or his experience and that her or his life matters even though they are no longer productive.

### Nurturing the Spirit

Persons can encounter God at any moment of life. We believe that the gentle voice of God speaks through our pain, our challenges, and our dreams of the future. Divine inspiration occurs through dreams and visions, and emerges even when persons are comatose. At the moment of death, God welcomes us and guides us to the next stage of the journey.

The ever-present God invites us to spiritual growth in every life situation. We can support the spiritual growth of dying persons by meditating with them, using spiritual practices, such as imaging the Divine Light, breath prayer, and centering prayer. We can sing songs, or read scriptures or other devotional material with them. We can simply be still in God's presence. This is holy ground, and God is here in the hospice, hospital, or bedroom.

The spirit is nurtured in spaciousness and silence. In quiet moments, the gentle light of God emerges. In touching and being touched, giving and receiving, the angel emerges from the boulder, transforming our inner life and external relationships.

**You can share God's love in circles of caring.** Living and dying are never solitary enterprises. At every stage of life, but most particularly when we are vulnerable and weak, we need kind words, faithful companions, and loving arms from womb to tomb. The spirit of shalom affirms that the communal nature of life goes beyond the family to embrace the circles of community and political life. The dying need the support of healing circles made up of compassionate friends from churches and temples, hospice care teams, nursing home staff, and home visitors. But beyond that, care for the dying has a political dimension in the accessibility of adequate health care for all persons at every stage of life and governmental policies that enable persons to respond creatively to issues of living and dying. The politics of compassion challenge us to create social and governmental structures that promote health and wholeness through economic justice, cost effective medical care for all, support of families dealing with medical crises, and adequate end of life care. We need a transformed vision of medicine that embraces high touch and high tech, complementary health care, and spiritual growth. The dying process can still be an opportunity for personal growth and spiritual transformation. A truly healing medicine can ease the pain and promote the comfort necessary for creative spiritual growth. Though compassion is a hands-on enterprise, healthy institutions nurture creative and supportive care giving for the vulnerable, helpless, dying, and their families.

**We can lovingly say our good-byes.** One of the hardest things a person can do is to say "good-bye" to a loved one, knowing that this will be quite possibly the last time. When Diane said "good-bye" to her ninety-one year old mother, her grief was overwhelming. Though her mother was a shell of her former self, Diane remembered the two of them going shopping, reading bedtime stories, walking in the woods, and discussing religious and philosophical questions. Even though Diane was an expert in issues related to death and dying, this still was new ground for her. "It wasn't somebody else's family I was dealing with now, it was my own. In the back of my mind were all the things I had said in lectures and counsel to families, but now it was *my* mom, and I wanted to run away."

In our good-byes, we experience again the mutuality of relationships—we receive as we give. What we share comes back to us. Though her mom could barely hear her, Diane said, "I love you, Mom. It's ok to let go, if you want. God is waiting for you. Dad is waiting for you too."

We can say "good-bye" to our loved ones, whether or not they are conscious. Both narrative accounts and medical experience report that persons in comas can often remember conversations and events, when they return to consciousness. We believe that, regardless of our mental condition, there is a part of each person that is always attuned to Love—the love of God and the love of others. The comatose are not merely "dead weight" or "lifeless carcasses"; deep within them, the voice of God whispers messages of love; hidden beneath their somnolence an angel is listening.

In saying our "good-byes," we need to be prepared to listen as well. Our dying friends and family still may have a story to tell. We need to hear their words of love. On the last day of her life, Janet's thirty year old daughter Kim, dying of leukemia, roused from consciousness long enough to say, "Mom and Dad, I love you. Thanks for everything."

Looking back, Janet remembers her daughter's words as "the greatest gift Kim and God could give me was that moment of love." Just as Rabbi Eleazer spoke of the need for repentance as a daily practice, we also need to take time each day to share words of love and gratitude. Our good-byes are the invitation to a greater "hello" that we will receive in God's eternal reign of shalom.

## An End and a Beginning

In his classic account of one man's dying process, *The Death of Ivan Illych,* Leo Tolstoy tells of the death and rebirth of a self-centered, narcissistic, upwardly mobile professional. Although he had fulfilled his professional and social obligations, made a good living, and purchased an upscale home for his family, Ivan's impending death brings about a spiritual crisis. As he looks back on his pleasant and successful life, Ivan asks himself, "was this the real thing?" He wonders if somehow, in rising to the top of his profession, he lost touch with the wonder and beauty of life. In the loneliness of his reflections, he cries out, "I want to live!" However, beneath his cries, he hears a whisper, "do you want to live as you did before?" In that question, Ivan hears the voice of God and his own deepest self.

Imprisoned by the mutual charade of denial and deception that had characterized his life and now contaminated his dying, Ivan fell into despair. Though he tries to defend his life as being "good enough" because of his income and place in society, he knows that there is nothing to defend. In his own "life review," he realized that he had been a failure at love and faith.

In the final days of his life, Ivan lets go of the need to defend himself. He knows his life is a mess and that there is virtually nothing he can do to make up for lost time. In his weakness, he reaches out to his family for the first time. He accepts the grace that can overcome our guilt and transform our imperfection into interdependence. Though his family cannot understand his words, his effort is enough to transform Ivan's soul. Though his physician and family believe that he is dying in utter agony, Ivan has finally found the peace that his quest for power and wealth could not achieve. He is no longer afraid of death and, though no one notices it, Ivan has finally learned to live. As he takes his last breath, Ivan falls into the abyss, but discovers the abyss he had feared is luminous. There is no darkness and death as the Divine Light guides him toward the next steps in his journey.

Yes, we are the dying taking care of the dying. That shock can shrink our spirit or awaken us to our stature as God's children. In companionship with the Creator of light and darkness, we can face our darkness and fear, woundedness and pain. We can forgive and let go, and say "good-bye" to those we love. A Holy Light and Gentle Touch, and a community of fellow pilgrims, surrounds us as we venture into the frontier that awaits our coming.

# CHAPTER FOUR

# *Living through Loss*

The story is told of a woman who came to Gautama the Buddha, carrying the body of her recently deceased child. Distraught with grief, she begged the holy man to restore her son to life. The Buddha promised he would revive her child, if she met only one condition—the woman needed to bring him a mustard seed that came from a family that had never lost a parent, child, spouse, sibling, or beloved animal to death. Hours later the bereaved mother returned, ready to go on with her life, for she had discovered the universality of grief. In facing her loss, she discovered a spiritual path in the midst of suffering.

In his profound record of his own experience of bereavement, *A Grief Observed,* Christian author C. S. Lewis speaks of grief as "like a long valley where any bend may reveal a totally new landscape."[1] In his inner dialogue with his recently deceased wife Joy, Lewis notes that "I had my miseries, not hers; she had hers, not mine. The end of hers would be the coming of age of mine."[2]

Though the experience of grief is unique to each person, the reality of grief is universal and unavoidable. Grief is occasioned by the loss of anything that is significant to our lives. Whether or not we are aware of it at the time, each one of us constantly lives with the reality of grief. Loss is both a metaphysical and relational necessity. Without the perpetual perishing of life, we could not grow. Novelty would be stifled by the burden of the past. The transformation we long for requires the death of past stabilities. Without strong bonds of love, tears would never flow. Without the comfort of the familiar, uneasiness over change would not occur.

A child tentatively begins her first day of school, and her father tearfully watches her recede into the distance, knowing that her new freedom means the end of one life and the beginning of another for both parent and child. A popular eighth grader starts all over again in high school, having to prove himself all over again with new peers and instructors. Phone bills soar when a child goes away to college, and at graduation that same child grieves over the anticipated changes that will occur in his relationships to the peers whose presence has been his polestar for the past four years. Parents divorce and their children's lives are plunged into emotional and financial turmoil. Elders bemoan the loss of hearing, sight, and energy that frequently accompanies the joys of longevity. Grief is an essential companion in our passage from one stage of life to the next in the adventure of spiritual evolution.

Nevertheless, for most of us, the greatest grief involves the death of spouse, child, parent, partner, or soul friend. With the death of an intimate loved one, an important part of our lives is lost forever. Our beloved friends and family members have been the architects of our soul making adventure in this lifetime. Their words and deeds have shaped our day-to-day experience, long-term values, and future hopes. A dynamic and eternal thread of love joins us our spirits that cannot be severed by our deaths. Yet with their deaths the cord of love is frayed and transformed. While we still have memories of our loved ones, the real and embodied presence is gone—dialogue has faded, touch lost forever, the familiar voice a distant echo, personal and intimate companionship a thing of the past.

Our experience of grief is grounded in the holy connectedness of life. Without loving interdependence, there would be no grief. The metaphysics of love is also the catalyst for the reality of bereavement. In speaking of the concrete reality of grief, C. S. Lewis notes:

> For all pairs of lovers without exception, bereavement is a universal and integral part of our experience of love. It follows marriage as normally as marriage follows courtship or as autumn follows summer. It is not a truncation of the process but one of its phases; not the interruption of the dance, but the next figure.[3]

Judaism and Christianity affirm the essential nature of relationships to the abundant life we seek. Life aims at shalom, or holy relatedness, between humans, the nonhuman world, and the Divine. In reflecting of the interdependence of life, Genesis notes, "it is not good [that a person] be alone" (Gen. 2:18).

Judaism and Christianity do not counsel withdrawal from the world of relationships, but commitment to the loving relationships of parent, child, friend, and life partner, as essential to our spiritual fulfillment. While times of spiritual retreat are essential to our growth, personal wholeness is a creative synthesis of reflection and action, silence and speech, solitude and community. Grief is not denied or avoided but seen as an essential part of God's intricately woven world of relationships. Those who do not love cannot grieve. Moreover, those who are unable to love can never understand the Divine passion for the world. Our grief is a reflection of the Divine grief over the pain and loss in the world.

The story is told of wise religious leader whose disciple discovered him crying in his study. "Why are you crying, teacher?" the student asked. "I thought wisdom meant detachment from emotions." The wise one replied, "When I am happy, I smile. When I am sad, I cry. Today, my dearest friend has died, and I honor our friendship with my tears."

The greatest spiritual leaders are persons whose emotional and intellectual lives are spacious in their inclusion of as much reality as can be embraced without losing their personal center. As a young man, the shepherd-warrior David, who was to become the greatest of Israel's kings, mourned when his beloved soul friend Jonathan was killed in battle. Later in life, the mighty king was brokenhearted at the death of his rebellious son Absalom. The Savior Jesus was moved to tears when he looked upon the grave of his dear friend Lazarus. No doubt Jesus was touched not only by his own pain, but also by the anguish of his dearest friends Mary and Martha. Though the Gospel story speaks of Jesus raising Lazarus from the dead, even the promise of eternal life cannot anesthetize the pain of loss. As he looked toward his death on the cross, Jesus no doubt anticipated the pain his male and female disciples would feel at his own death. We suspect that he also mourned the severing of the ties that had bound them together as rabbi and disciples.

Fidelity to God and spiritual growth mean greater openness to experience in all its dimensions. Joyful awareness is built upon embracing the totality of life, including moments of celebration and sorrow. In addressing a persecuted first century church, the early Christian leader Paul of Tarsus counseled believers to "not grieve as others do who have no hope" (1 Thess. 4:13). In a world in which life entails loss, and creativity requires letting go of the familiar past, we need to discover wholeness amid the unavoidable realities of grief.

When his wife of forty-four years, Sheila, suddenly died of a heart attack, Abe wondered if he could make it on his own. She had been his soul mate and other half since they met in their first year of college. Together, they had traveled the world, given lectures, and led workshops. "What will life be without her?" Abe confessed to his friends and family. For the first few weeks, Abe could barely get out of bed. The future that they had planned together after they both would retire had been obliterated in just a few moments.

Though he admits to have sleepwalked through the first weeks after her death, Abe remembers being consoled by services at his temple, where he heard the proclamation of God's eternal love and fidelity. Resting in the familiar rituals, Abe knew that in God's eternity Sheila lived on. His community of family and friends from the temple, university, and neighborhood surrounded Abe with their love. Barely able to boil hot water prior to his wife's death, Abe received simple recipes from his children and friends as well as casseroles, desserts, and soups for the journey ahead.

The first year was the most difficult. Abe admits that her presence was everywhere. Each day, he expected to see Sheila working in her study or digging in their garden. Several times a day Abe found himself calling home from his office at the university before lunch and prior to his departure from work as he had done for nearly four decades. The phone rang and rang, but no one was present to answer. With great regret, Abe finally taped over his wife's cheery message on their home answering machine.

Amid the grief of that first year, Abe found hope in the community of friends who wrote letters, made phone calls, and invited him to dinner and social engagements. Even when he said he was too tired or not in the mood, Abe felt loved and connected to the world beyond himself. He was grateful that they took the initiative in reaching out to him. Each week at temple, he recited the traditional prayers for the dead and committed himself to choosing life as a way of honoring Sheila's vital and creative spirit. The Jewish religious holidays took on new meaning as Abe came to experience the profound interplay of human mortality and Divine eternity.

Five years after his wife's death, Abe admits that sometimes it is still difficult to return to his solitary home. Although he has not yet chosen to remarry, he now enjoys the company of couples as well as his male and female companions. "At first, I wasn't sure I could make it, but the comfort and challenge of friends, my faith, and God's presence in my life pushed me ahead. I wanted to be worthy of my grief. I needed to choose life for myself, my children and grandchildren, and my God. My family and friends, and especially my college students, needed to see that a person could grieve and yet go on with her or his life. In my mourning, I found a new vocation—that of survivor and mentor of those who grieve."

Abe has become a leader of the grief support group at his university and often counsels students and staff of all faiths in dealing with deep feelings brought about by death, divorce, homesickness, and failure. In his darkest hours, Abe was nurtured by the realism of Psalm 23. In living with the Psalm's twin images of threat and security, Abe affirmed "the only way I could find healing was to go through the valley of death, not around it. I found God in the darkness and experienced God's abundant care in the presence of my depression and loss. Now, out of my grief, I can become a healing companion for others."

While many persons find solace in their faith, the experience of loss can also challenge our belief in God or awaken us to new images of the Divine. Deeply committed to God, C. S. Lewis still profoundly felt the absence of the Holy One following his beloved wife Joy's death. In anguished words that can only come from the pen of a believer, Lewis—like Job two thousand years before him—challenged his previous images of the divine-human relationship:

> Meanwhile, where is God? This is one of the most disquieting symptoms. When you are happy, so happy that you have no sense of needing Him, so happy that you are tempted to feel His claims upon you as an interruption, if you remember yourself and turn to him with gratitude and praise, you will be—or so it feels— welcomed with open arms. But go to Him when your need is desperate, when all other help is vain, and what

do you find? A door slammed in your face, and a sound of bolting and double bolting on the inside. After that, silence…Why is He so present a commander in our time of prosperity and so very absent in a time of trouble?[4]

In the spirit of the loneliness of Jesus on the cross and the anguish of author of Psalm 22, countless bereaved persons cry out, "My God, my God, why have you forsaken me?" In its universality, grief—like death—may deaden our spirits. However, it also may the open the door to a deeper experience of Divinity and a greater awareness of the radical wonder of each day. We may discover new hope and new love in the midst of the anguish of grief. Like the prophet Isaiah, we may discover a verdant and vital branch, growing from what once was a gnarled stump. Out of our sorrow and weakness, we may experience the strength that comes from experiencing the love of others and the companionship of the Holy One.

## The Landscape of Grief

How we respond to grief can be a matter of life and death. In the profound interconnectedness of life, our response to loss affects our physical, emotional, spiritual, and relational well-being. Following the death of a spouse, the one left behind, especially the husband, is at greater risk of hospitalization for serious physical illness, depression, and emotional turmoil. Mortality rates skyrocket in the year following the death of a spouse, particularly among men. Significant loss disorients and destabilizes persons to the center of their being, but within the experience of loss, we can also discover new vitality and an unexpected future.

While each person responds to loss in her or his own way, there are certain universal characteristics of the grief experience. Awareness of these typical responses to grief is essential to the healing process, initially, because awareness liberates us from the fear that during our time of bereavement, we are losing our minds or are absolutely alone in our sense of loss. In discovering our common experience, we claim our partnership with countless other grievers and find the healing resources to support our companions as they walk through the valley of loss.[5]

An ancient Jewish ritual involves the rending, or tearing, of garments just before a funeral. Grief, like a tear in a coat, dress, or pair of slacks, wounds us deeply and permanently. Though we may stitch up our clothes and experience the healing of our grief, the wound still remains. To honor this loss and the pain that emerges in the most unexpected situations, the torn garment is always left unrepaired.

As we ponder the healing process for those who grieve, we acknowledge that we never fully "get over" the losses we have experienced, nor do we ever really want to! They remain in our unconscious and shape our future relationships. In the interplay of loss and celebration, our lives are filled with fond memories as well as feelings of pain. Further, the uniqueness of human experience demands that we recognize that healing is an organic, rather than linear, process in which there is no prescribed order of experience. We do an injustice to ourselves and others by demanding that only one particular path toward wholeness be followed.

For many persons, the initial stage of grief involves the experience of *shock* and *denial*. As she walked the peaceful streets of Potomac, Maryland, on the evening of September 11, 2001, Louisa felt as if she were in a dream. "How could such a terrible day be followed by such a lovely evening? This cannot be happening to our nation!" she pondered in the silence of a plane-free sky.

When Maria lost her job at an investment firm during the recession of 2002, she had to pinch herself just to believe she was no longer an employee at the firm that had been her vocational home for ten years. "Intellectually I know that I no longer work for the firm, but each morning I start dressing for work as if I have somewhere to go. I can't believe this happened to me."

Shock and denial, like anesthesia, provide initial relief from the harsh realities of life. We need time to embrace the losses that confront us. Often what looks like serenity is the emotional concussion that occurs after a significant loss. Eventually, we may move from shock and denial to *affirmation, acceptance,* and *creative transformation.*

Grief is a profoundly *emotional experience.* In the wake of a significant loss, we may cry, shake, lament, or moan in anguish. Our very being cries out at the pain of being separated from someone or something essential to our lives. When his mother died unexpectedly, Stewart broke down for the first time in his adult life. As one sob followed another, he felt as if his tears would never end. In the months ahead, Stewart learned to see his tears as a blessing, a visible sign of his love for his mother. Five years later, Stewart admits, "I still cry from time to time. My eyes moisten when I'm watching a sentimental movie or remember something special Mom and I did together. But I am grateful for the tears I still shed for Mom. They remind me of how much her love meant to me." Medical research has indicated that tears, like laughter, are good medicine. When we cry, our bodies secrete enzymes that contribute to our overall well-being. Spiritual traditions see tears as a gift of God, and the sign of a love that cares enough to reveal its pain.

Life aims at the future. Each moment creatively integrates past, present, and future. As the house for our hopes and dreams, the future lures us forward with the promise of fulfillment and adventure. When our images of the future—a career in our chosen field, an ongoing relationship, the fulfillment of a dream—are shattered, we are physically and emotionally depressed. While *the depression of grief* should not be confused with clinical depression, often the symptoms are similar—laziness and lack of energy, inability to look beyond the present moment, and flatness of emotion. When she received the word that she was passed over for a major promotion, Emily could barely get out of bed for the first week. Usually vivacious and extroverted, she wanted to crawl in a hole until the pain of disappointment passed. In responding to his own grief, the psalmist cries out, "Why are you cast down, O my soul, and why are you disquieted within me?" (Ps. 43:5a).

Though the depression of grief will eventually pass, initially there seems to be no way out of the pain we are experiencing. New life will emerge, but only after we have experienced the labor pains of depression and hopelessness. Before we experience a new connection with the future and its possibilities, we must journey through the realm of loneliness and disconnection. Sometimes, with the author of Psalm 43, we must trust the unseen future and hope against hope that a healing path will open up in the darkness.

With all his concern about the future, the psalmist imagines the lifting of pain and grief, "Hope in God; for I shall again praise [God], / my help and my God" (Ps. 43:5b).

Along with depression and emotional release, grief often manifests itself in *physical illness.* In the words of the psalmist, we are "fearfully and wonderfully made" (Ps. 139:14). Mind, body, spirit, and relationships are woven together inseparably. A change in one dimension of life, for example, our emotional relationship with another, leads to changes in every other aspect of life. In times of bereavement, we question the goodness of God and the trustworthiness of the universe. Mental focus often deteriorates. Grief may even lead to changes in our physical condition.

Following his wife's death, Drew experienced severe neck and headaches. He also missed the loving touch of his wife of twenty years. "I miss her most in my body. The back rubs, the hand in mine, and the intimacy of sexuality," he still admits two years after her death. "I may remarry, but Maureen will always be my first love."

Even the best of relationships are imperfect and broken. The very fact of our unique individuality leads to what the poet Kahlil Gibran described as "spaces in our togetherness." When a loved dies, we can no longer make amends for times of neglect or poorly chosen words. We can no longer say "I love you" or

"I'm sorry" directly to them. We often feel *guilt* that we did not do more in their final days or missed opportunities to nurture their physical or spiritual well-being. Our imperfections stand ready to judge and convict us.

Though she was a devoted daughter who visited or called her mother daily, faithfully managed her mother's finances, and compassionately supervised her health care, Lydia felt that she should have done more to make her mother's final days comfortable and worry free. She felt especially guilty that she was caught in a traffic jam at the exact moment her mother died.

Heavily burdened by guilt, Lydia sought out her pastor for spiritual advice. Her burden was lifted when her pastor led her through imaginative healing exercises in which Lydia could tell her mother "I love you" for the last time. Her pastor reminded Lydia that her mother was not alone when she died. The Loving God who had been with her at conception received her with open arms at her death. Now, when she feels pangs of guilt, Lydia remembers her pastor's words, "You were a great daughter. The better a child you are, the more present you are with your parents, the more mistakes you make. But what would your mother's life have been like without you? Remember, Lydia, that you have children of your own and a husband who needs your support. You have to trust that when you could not be with your mother, other loving arms were there—your brother, your Mom's friends from church, and the home care staff. But most of all God was with her each moment as well."

Grief opens up an avalanche of feelings, many of which would embarrass us if they were made public. When a relative is ill over a long period of time, we may in our fatigue and pain wish that they would die quickly. Other times, especially when death is protracted, we feel guilty because we do not sob or moan in pain when death finally occurs. We forget that for years we have preparing spiritually, emotionally, and physically for the death of our loved one. We have been grieving all along. Many of our tears have already been shed, although we may break down months after the funeral or when we realize that there is a void in our lives that was once filled by the habitual tasks of caring for a dying spouse or parent. The relief we feel is a natural and holy response to our constant care in the past and our ongoing anticipation of our loved one's eventual death.

Among the feelings that are often released when a loved one dies, *anger* is most devastating. We cannot imagine how we could be angry at the deceased. Nevertheless, in the dynamic relatedness of life, the death of another, especially a parent or spouse, changes everything. We are no longer someone's child, spouse, or mother. Our financial situation may change radically. We may have to assume new roles at home. We may be angry at the departed because of "unfinished business"—our spouse or parent may have neglected or abused us intentionally or unintentionally; their behaviors (smoking, alcoholism, overeating) may have led to premature disability and death; their death may have occurred at particularly painful time of estrangement. Even though our loved one may not have intended to die, we have been left behind! This feeling of anger may be especially strong when a parent, child, or spouse commits suicide, and prematurely cuts off any possibilities for direct and mutual communication or relational healing.

When we feel guilt over our anger at a deceased loved one or at those whose parents or spouses are still living, we can take consolation with the image of God's loving omniscience found in Psalm 139:

> O [God], you have searched me and known me.
> You know when I sit down and when I rise up;
> > you discern my thoughts from far away.
> You search out my path and my lying down,
> > and are acquainted with all my ways.
> Even before a word is on my tongue,
> > O [God], you know it completely.
> You hem me in behind and before,
> > and lay your hand upon me.

Such knowledge is too wonderful for me;
 it is so high I cannot attain it. (Ps. 139:1–6)

Divine knowledge enables us to see ourselves for what we
are in all our stature as well as our small mindedness. Known
completely by God, we can face the worst in ourselves with
forgiveness of the past and hope in the future.

The Psalms are not for the fainthearted, nor do they
attempt to cover up the harsh realities of life or the ambiguity
of the human heart. Amid the majesty of Psalm 139, these
apparently incongruous words of anger express the healing
power of being fully known by God:

O that you would kill the wicked, O God,
 and that the bloodthirsty would depart from me—
those who speak of you maliciously,
 and lift themselves up against you for evil!
Do I not hate those who hate you, O LORD?
 And do I not loathe those who rise up against you?
I hate them with perfect hatred;
I count them my enemies. (Ps. 139:19–22)

There are times when anger against the deceased is a
natural and just response to our pain and the evil perpetrated
against others. As he walked the halls of the Theology
Department at Georgetown University on the morning of
September 11th, one of Bruce's colleagues, otherwise a gentle
pacifist, confided, "right now, I want to nuke the al Qaida!"

Our anger cannot become holy passion for justice for
ourselves and for others until we acknowledge its reality and
impact on our lives. When we place our anger in God's hands,
the Divine Alchemist transforms anger into understanding,
power, and the quest for justice for the oppressed and abused.
As he pours out his anger to God, the psalmist's spirit once
again soars into the spacious realm of Divine Companionship.
The psalmist knows that even if he cannot let go of his malice,
God has sufficient stature to embrace his anger with healing
love:

> Search me, O God, and know my heart;
>    test me and know my thoughts.
> See if there is any wicked way in me,
>    and lead me in the way everlasting.
>                              (Ps. 139:23–24)

In the long valley of grief, sometimes we worry that we are losing our minds. We *panic and become anxious* as our thoughts race through memories of deceased. We wonder if we'll ever be able to regain our mental focus. We're unsettled by the "phantom limb syndrome"—though the beloved is absent, we still feel her or his presence. Everything from hearing "our song," the sight of a favorite chair, the scent of a familiar perfume or cologne is a reminder of what we once had and what is gone forever. After his wife's death, David began to doubt his mental well being when he discovered that he called his wife's office number virtually every day for the first few weeks after her death. Mercifully for David, his wife's former secretary was a widow and remembered that his daily ritual was to call his wife at work during his mid-afternoon coffee break. She understood the power of habit and ritual which goes well beyond the death of friends and loved ones.

Following the loss of a beloved friend or family member, we are often reluctant to immerse ourselves in new relationships. After her dog of fifteen years died, Elaine told well-meaning friends not to give her a puppy. "I'm not sure I can take the pain of losing a pet again!" mourned the seventy-year-old widow.

In a similar fashion, following his divorce after twenty years of marriage, Simon resisted dating for nearly two years. "I'm not ready to invest myself in a relationship yet. The wounds of my divorce are still too great to bear. I'm a little gun-shy and don't want to risk the pain of another relational failure."

Like any wound, the healing process of grief cannot be accelerated beyond what is optimal for the person involved. At the right time, Elaine found she could open her heart to a puppy and now walks jauntily with her lively and mischievous Golden Retriever Patrick. After his sabbatical from dating, Simon began to participate in a singles group at his church. For a while, he only went out in groups to "safe" activities such as dinners, plays, and sporting events. Eventually he found new love and has remarried a member of the singles' group.

When a loved one dies or is separated from us, we discover that life will never be the same. The future looks uncertain and frightening. However, spiritual seekers discover that God is luring them forward to new horizons even in unsettled times. As the Divine Companion proclaimed to brokenhearted exiles in Babylon, "For surely I know the plans I have for you.... plans for welfare and not for harm, to give you a future with hope" (Jer. 29:11).

There is no exact timetable to the healing of grief. God moves gently through our brokenness, awakening us to new possibilities, giving us the hope of abundant life after painful loss. Eventually, for most persons, the valley of grief opens us to a broad horizon of *hope*. Even though life remains hard, now we know that we will make it. While we will always feel the loss of our loved one, we discover that life still has adventures and surprises ahead of us. Death is real. Loss is always a possibility for us in the future. Nevertheless, in partnership with the Divine Artist, we can fashion angels from the boulders of our lives.

## The Fellow Sufferer Who Understands

The reality of grief and loss may be especially difficult for those who believe in God. Many of us feel that our faith and spiritual disciplines immunize us from the tragedies of life. We are overwhelmed when a spouse dies, a partner leaves us, or a child commits suicide. "This can't be happening to me!" we moan. "I've done the right things. I've meditated, practiced positive visualizations, said my prayers, and gone to religious services. I say affirmations each day and practice random acts of kindness on a regular basis." What is more unsettling to persons of faith is the emotional pain itself. We often feel that our spiritual growth will deliver us from anger, guilt, tears, and loneliness when tragedy occurs. We doubt our own faith, believing it simply to be a "house of cards" unable to take the storms of life, when we fall into depression or falter in our optimism, just like everyone else. We forget that authentic spirituality opens us to a wider world of experience and that spiritual growth is accompanied by greater sensitivity to our own suffering and the suffering of others. At such moments, we are challenged to treat ourselves with the same compassion that we would treat another person following a significant loss. We need to be reminded that the Holy One loves the "lost lamb" as much as the ones safely protected in the pen, and that God's intimate care embraces us just as much in our pain as in our joy (Lk. 15:1–7).

Still, unhealthy visions of God plague us and may plunge us into despair, guilt, or impotence. We need a God big enough to face our grief, fear, and doubt with us. A God, who is too small or whose love is too limited, cannot comfort us when our lives are out of control. Though God seemed absent to C. S. Lewis in his grief, Lewis still sought to discover a God who could bring healing to his grief:

> Not that I am (I think) in much danger of ceasing to believe in God. The real danger is to believe such dreadful things about Him. The conclusion I dread is not, "So there's no God after all," but "So this is what God's really like. Deceive yourself no longer." Our elders submitted and said, "Thy will be done." How often had bitter resentment been stifled through sheer terror and an act of love—yes, in every sense, an act— put on to hide the operation.[6]

Authentic spirituality lives in the creative tension of Psalm 22 and Psalm 23. The one who cries out "my God, my God, why have you forsaken me?" discovers in the midst of his hopelessness that God's companionship is the ground of healing. In the darkest valley, the Divine Shepherd "leads me beside still waters" and "restores my soul."

God's companionship heals our grief. Emmanuel, "God with us," embraces the totality of our lives. Our deepest fears and greatest anguish find a home in God's loving embrace. We are never alone in our suffering. God comforts us even as God challenges us to embrace the new life that lies beyond our suffering and loss.

God does not cause our grief. God did not take away the loved ones, who are victims of the senseless killings in America's inner cities. God did not unleash the cancer cells, the blood clot, or the explosion of the space shuttle, or cause the planes to crash into the World Trade Center. God is present in our tears and fears. Nevertheless, the ever-present God is also always active to bring healing in the most painful situations. Within the cry of creation and our own painful moans, God is gently inviting us toward wholeness and healing. The God who does *not* cause evil constantly invites us to become God's companions in the transformation of our pain and the pain of the world. Divine goodness calls us to place our grief in a wider perspective and move forward with our lives one step at a time rather than succumbing to self-pity and victimization. Within the labyrinth of grief, the Holy One is at work to enable us to become persons of spiritual stature, whose light rises from loss with hope in tomorrow and comfort for a suffering world.

# CHAPTER FIVE

# Mending the Broken Connection

In world characterized by dynamic interdependence, our experience of loss encompasses the personal and communal dimensions of life. While we are ultimately responsible for our own healing process, none of us is ever healed alone. Our quest to reclaim life's vitality is nurtured by the rituals of our faith traditions and the companionship of loved ones. These creative healing circles enable us to face the profound disconnectedness and emptiness of our grief while affirming the goodness of life. We learn to embrace grief and hope as we take our first tentative steps toward new life. Those whom we've loved can never be replaced—there will always be a rip in the garment of life—but we can experience greater vitality and appreciation for our unique and precious lives by committing ourselves to growing in spirit through ritual and personal transformation, even when life is frayed.

## Transforming Rituals

Grief plunges us into unknown territory. Like the intrepid adventurers Abraham and Sarah, we wonder if God will be our companion in the wilderness that lies ahead. Torn between the grief of leaving their familiar home and the hope of a glorious, new homeland, Sarah and Abraham erected altars at every stop to remind them that even in the wilderness of uncertainty God was their guide and protector. God would make a pathway when no way ahead was visible.

In times of sorrow and loss, rituals enable us to navigate uncharted paths into the future. Historically, religious rituals provide comfort, security, and challenge in life's transitional moments. When the realities of life challenge us to claim a new identity, rituals affirm that the One who guided us in the past will lead us into the future and that we will have the resources to respond creatively to the next stage of life, whether it be young adulthood, marriage, parenting, dying, grieving, or living alone for the first time since our wedding day. In these moments of pain and celebration, rituals remind us that we are not alone. We are part of an intricately woven community of fellow sojourners who share our joys and sorrows.

While many persons today disparage rituals as cold, lifeless, and routine, healing rituals transform our lives when they reflect the fullness of our emotional and spiritual lives and the support of the communities in which we dwell. Just as twenty-first century faith is dynamic, creative, and eclectic, life-transforming rituals join ancient wisdom with the global spirituality of our time. The stability of tradition is synthesized with the dynamism of new spiritual practices to create a lively circle of healing.

When Bruce's father, Everett, died, the rituals following his death were an epiphany for Bruce and his family. During those holy days, Bruce chose the spirit of receptivity, embarking on the difficult task of being a receiver rather than a giver during the initial mourning period. At the graveside and at the church, words of comfort and praise were spoken:

> The LORD is my shepherd, I shall not want.
>
> [God] makes me lie down in green pastures;

[God] leads me beside still waters;
    [God] restores my soul.
[God] leads me in the right paths
    for [the divine] name's sake.
Even though I walk through the darkest valley,
    I fear no evil;
for you are with me;
    your rod and your staff—they comfort me.
                (Ps. 23:1–4)

In the congregation where Bruce's father had worshipped for nearly forty years, songs of praise and gratitude also filled the air:

Amazing grace! How sweet the sound
that saved a wretch like me!
I once was lost, but now am found;
was blind, but now I see.
Through many dangers, toils, and snares,
I have already come;
'Tis grace hath brought me safe thus far,
and grace will lead me home.
When we've been there ten thousand years,
bright shining as the sun,
we've no less days to sing God's praise
than when we first begun.[1]

During the eulogies for his father, Bruce was reminded of his father's gentle spirit and commitment to his faith and church. But he also learned new and surprising things about his father's life. He learned that although his parents initially opposed the sharing of their church building with the Metropolitan Community Church, a gay and lesbian worshipping community, they eventually became great supporters of the church and its pastor. As his family dabbed tears from their eyes, they were filled with gratitude to the Source of all Life and Beauty for Everett's life, the closeness of their family, and the loving community of faith that accompanied Everett throughout his illness and dying.

Progressive and traditional Christianity and Judaism share the belief that the rituals surrounding the death of a loved one respond to our need for order, community, and transformation in times of loss and transition. They reconnect us to the Divine healing presence that moves through worship, touch, friendship, and personal growth. In healing the broken connection between the living and the dead, rituals bring healing to those who mourn and may even contribute to the spiritual evolution of the recently deceased. Rituals enable us to let go of reality as it once was, so that we may reaffirm our relationship to our loved ones and to the future that beckons us forward.

Our awakening to the ongoing process of creative transformation, from which each life arises and to which each life returns is portrayed in the following story of Rabbi Meir and his wife Beruriah:

> On Sabbath afternoon, while he was teaching in the House of Study, both of Rabbi Meir's sons died. His wife, Beruriah, waited until the Sabbath was over to tell him in order not to dampen his Sabbath joy. After Rabbi Meir had eaten, she asked him, "Some time ago, a friend gave me some jewels for safekeeping. Today that person demands them back. What should I do?" Rabbi Meir unhesitatingly responded, "You must return the jewels." Then she led the Rabbi to the room where their children lay dead. "These are the jewels I must return," she said. Overcome with grief, Rabbi Meir repeated the words of Job, "God gave and the Eternal has taken back. Blessed be the name of the Holy One."[2]

While we do not believe that God takes away the lives of our loved ones, we affirm that in the midst of our grief, God provides us with rituals, community, and spiritual insight to help us face the challenges of living with loss.

Ironically, letting go and embracing are intimately connected. Grief is occasioned by the shock and pain of separation. The healing of grief involves the affirmation of that deep separation in the context of the deeper connectedness of God's love. Just as transformation requires destruction, healing requires acknowledging the finality of death and separation. Awareness of death's finality opens the door to new life and the possibility of an evolving spiritual relationship with the deceased. Our creative response to death involves living through a number of nonlinear moments.

## When Death Occurs

Even when the death of a loved one is anticipated, we initially experience a sense of shock and disbelief. As we view our loved one's body or experience her or his final breaths, we are astounded by the mysterious transition between life and death, and this phase of life and the next. We know that the loved one is more than her or his inert body. While the spirit that gave life has departed, or is in the process of departing, the dead body of a spouse, child, parent, or friend, is holy ground. Something of their personality and spiritual identity still remains embodied in the lifeless corpse, even when the doors of communication have apparently been closed.

Mystical Judaism holds in tension both life and death at such holy moments. According to the Jewish mystical tradition, the spirit that animated a person during life does not immediately depart from the body at death, but gradually weans itself from the world of the flesh in order to prepare for its next spiritual adventures. In the ecology of life, there is a thread of love that joins the living and the dead. Even as the spirit leaves our world, mystical Judaism asserts that the spirit needs our support in order to let go of the physical body and enter the postmortem world with greater peace. As grief-stricken as we may feel, we still have a responsibility to prayerfully support those who have just died.

Traditional Christianity has been humble, by comparison to Jewish mysticism, in its reflections on the postmortem journey of the recently deceased. Still, the image of the "communion of the saints" affirms that there is a connection between the faithful deceased and those who remain. According to some Christian traditions, the faithful deceased, often described as saints, intercede on our behalf before the Holy One and may influence affairs in our world. Further, the traditional Roman Catholic belief in Purgatory and the prayerful influence we may have on those who have recently died suggests that the door may not be shut from our side as well. The Christian tradition speaks of Jesus visiting the realm of the dead to preach the good news of salvation in the period between his crucifixion and resurrection. While we must avoid literal understandings of the postmortem journey, global and cross-cultural evidence points to the possibility of some form of communication and interaction between the living and the deceased. Following his wife's death, C. S. Lewis reflected on the grief that the dying may feel at their separation from their previous life.

> If, as I can't help suspecting, the dead also feel the pains of separation (and this may be one of their purgatorial sufferings), then for both lovers and all pairs of lovers without exception, bereavement is a universal and integral part of our experience of love.[3]

In traditional Christianity and Judaism, care for the recently deceased was often left to the family and friends. While this is seldom possible in the modern hospital setting, certain hospices and hospitals allow the family to sit with the deceased for a period of time following her or his death. This gentle and unhurried time blesses both the living and the dead. In the Christian tradition, this practice enables the living to say "goodbye" and face the reality of death before the cosmetic treatments of the funeral home. As we sit beside our beloved's still body, we affirm our pain at separation and our appreciation for the life force that has animated the one who lies before us. We may choose to speak authentic words of love to the deceased, sharing our gratitude for her or his role in our lives. If there is unfinished business, we may choose to use a forgiveness meditation to let go of any burden that may impede us, and possibly the deceased, in moving onward in our spiritual adventures. Regardless of our loved one's imperfections, we are challenged to forgive and be forgiven, and to let the beloved move onward in the companionship of the Eternal One.

In traditional Judaism, the body of the deceased is treated with great reverence. In the time immediately following death, the body is never left alone. A watcher remains with the body, prayerfully reciting the Psalms, and thus reassuring the family that the body is being lovingly cared for. In recent years, there has been a resurgence of Jewish burial societies, whose primary task is to say prayers and recite Psalms as the body is prepared for burial. Members of the burial society pray for the forgiveness of sins and the hope of lasting peace for the deceased. Following the *Taharah* ritual, they wash and purify the body, and dress it in a linen shroud, to facilitate the body's return to the earth from which it came. Finally, the body is placed in a plain, pine coffin, without nails, screws, and any other fasteners, as symbolic of the equality of all persons in death.

Traditional Judaism prohibits viewing the body before or at the funeral service. In contrast, many modern Christians, who choose to have viewings or open-casket funerals, affirm the importance of the "viewing" as an opportunity to experience the reality of death, pay respects to the deceased, and support those who grieve. The Christian practice of viewing affirms the communal nature of death and the sacredness of flesh, even as it allows one last physical contact with the deceased.

In both religious traditions, the time between death and the funeral or memorial service is seen as a holy time—a time for tears and remembering, a time to connect with loved ones while we begin to let go of the deceased, a time for hugs and loving support. During this time, apart from funeral arrangements, normal activities are suspended so that we can fully experience our loss and the significance of the deceased in our lives. In the midst of our pain, we are called to prayerful affirmation. We thank the Giver for the gift of life, embodied in our loved one. We rest in the eternity of God's love as we pray for our beloved's postmortem journey. We allow ourselves simply to receive the love and support of others without apology or excuse. In the ecology of life, we know that sometime in the future, we will be called upon to comfort others as they mourn their own losses.

### Funerals and Farewells

Though God is present and active in all times and places, certain moments and places become what the Celtic spiritual tradition has described as "thin places" in our experience of the Holy. In these "thin places," the temporal world is permeated by eternity, and the living and the dead experience communion.[4] These spiritual sanctuaries provide a safe place for persons in transition from one stage of life to another. Within their precincts, we can express our insecurity, vulnerability, anger, and emotional pain, and know that these are treasured and affirmed. One of the most powerful healing circles is the funeral or memorial service, where friends and family gather to experience the interplay of time and eternity in the presence of Divine Love. The words of greeting from the *Book of Worship* of the United Church of Christ proclaim the intersection of Divine and human love and healing that joins both Christians and Jews:

> Friends, we gather in the protective shelter of God's healing love. We are free to pour out our grief, release our anger, face our emptiness, and know that God cares. We gather here as God's people, conscious of others who have died, and of the frailty of our own existence on earth. We come to comfort and support one another in our common loss. We gather to hear God's word of hope that can drive away our despair and move us to offer God our praise.[5]

Funerals join grief and gospel, pain and good news, for those who have faith in the Eternal One. In traditional Jewish and Christian funeral and memorial services, the community gathers to pray, share, and support one another. In solidarity with those who grieve, we find strength in the recognition that we never walk alone. We celebrate the life of our loved one through eulogies and prayers of thanksgiving. We affirm that love casts out fear and that whatever is loved shares in God's eternal life. We recognize the loving ties that bind us with the deceased and place both our love and any guilt or anger we may feel in God's eternal care. As a time of spiritual examination, funerals remind us to recognize our own mortality and commit ourselves to the path of love, wonder, service, and gratitude.

The scriptures of our faith traditions call us to affirm that the Eternal is embodied in life and death. We are in God's hands in life and death. Hymns of faith and scriptural affirmations touch our emotions and join heart and mind in praise of the Eternal, whose love now guides and protects the one we love in the next stage of her or his adventure. As one Jewish prayer book affirms, God receives the deceased in her or his imperfection and welcomes her or him to God's realm of peace.

> Compassionate God, Eternal Spirit of the universe, God of forgiveness, mercy, and abounding loving-kindness, pardon his/her transgressions and grant perfect rest in the shadow of Your wings to _____, who has entered eternity. O God of compassion, remember him/her for all the meritorious deeds he/she did on earth. Open to him/her the gates of righteousness and light, the gates of mercy and grace. Let the departed find refuge in your eternal presence. Let his/her soul be bound up in the bond of eternal life. God is his/her inheritance. May he/she rest in peace.[6]

In traditional Jewish rituals and many Christian rituals, the lowering of the body in the ground at the gravesite proclaims the finality of death for the body. We are returned to the Great

Mother Earth, "from dust to dust." However, even as we lower the body into the ground, we affirm the eternal Light of God that will go forth beyond the grave. As a gravestone in Falls Church, Virginia, notes, "dust to dust and ashes to ashes was never said of the soul." As the Jewish graveside service ends, mourners recite the Burial Kaddish, glorifying God:

> Let the glory of God be extolled, let the Eternal's great name be magnified and sanctified in the world created according to the Divine will. May God's spiritual foundation soon prevail in our own day, in our own lives, and the life of Israel, and let us say, Amen.

> Let God's great name be blessed now and forever and ever. Let the name and the presence of the Blessed Holy One be praised, glorified, exalted, extolled, and honored, though the Almighty is beyond all praises, songs, and expressions that we utter, and let us say, Amen.

> For us and for everyone, may the abundance of peace and the promise of life's goodness come true and let us say, Amen.

> May the God, who causes the peace to reign in the high heavens, bring peace to us, to all Israel, and to everyone, and let us say, Amen.[7]

In that "thin place" where the living and dead find communion, we let go of the deceased and send them forward on their journey with our prayers. In the profoundly relational world in which God is present in all things, death cannot ultimately sever our relationship with the deceased or the impact that our lives may have on each other. While we cannot fully know the impact our prayers have on the dead, our prayers, affirmations, and visualizations bring peace to our hearts as we seek to be God's partners in supporting the afterlife journey of our loved ones. In the spirit of the traditional Song of Simeon from the Christian funeral service, we bid good-bye to the beloved and commit her or him to God's Loving Guidance and Care:

> Holy One, now let your servant go in peace;
> Your word has been fulfilled:
> my own eyes have seen the salvation
> which you have prepared in the sight of every people:
> a light to reveal you to the nations
> and the glory to your people Israel.[8]

## Seasons of Prayer and Remembrance

Our loved ones dwell forever in our hearts and minds. Frequently, our eyes mist when we think of them. We tell stories about them, many of which are humorous, to our friends and children. We most deeply miss them at certain occasions—holidays, weddings, bar and bat mitzvahs—and at certain places—a favorite restaurant, the symphony, or a walking trail we frequented. These moments join both grief and celebration—feelings of loss and affirmations of the wonder of this unique life.

In the Jewish tradition, the year after a loved one's death calls us to embark upon a journey of prayer, praise, and letting go. Following the funeral, the family and friends of the deceased engage in the traditional practice of "sitting shiva," a three to seven day period in which the mourners devote their energies to remembering and grieving over the deceased. Not confined to the immediate family, "sitting shiva" may involve scores of friends who come during the period following the funeral to pray, reminisce, and comfort. The presence of family and friends reminds the bereaved that life goes on and that they are surrounded by formal and informal communities of care. Traditionally, a memorial candle burns throughout this period of mourning. Symbolic of the spirit of the deceased, the memorial candle "raises the light" of the beloved by inspiring our prayers and good wishes for their spiritual journey.

Sitting shiva reminds us of the interplay between the personal and social dimensions of healing and salvation. Healing is never a private affair, but involves the loving care of a concerned community of friends and family. Mystical Judaism sees this period of mourning as an opportunity to support the spiritual adventure of the deceased. Mourners may open a spiritual pathway to communication with the recently deceased through prayer, affirmation of the need to let go of the earth, gratitude, and mutual forgiveness. Grief awakens a deeper perception of reality and a heightened sense of awareness, which may facilitate subtle communication with the deceased.

While not nearly as formal as Judaism, Christianity recognizes the need for caring communities through receptions, wakes, and dinners following the funeral as well as home visits to the bereaved, usually accompanied by desserts or casseroles. At its best this loving "casserole theology" reminds us that where there is food there is life and that we honor the dying by our commitment to live on with grace, dignity, and purpose.

In many ways, the year following a significant loss is the most difficult. Rituals and remembrances enable us to feel the depths of our sorrow even as we commit ourselves more fully to the ongoing realities of life. Again, ironically, the more we intentionally face our grief and remember our loved one, the easier the separation generally becomes over the long haul. Many grievers have discovered that letting go is the prelude to healthy connection with the one who has died. In the Jewish tradition, mourners continue throughout the first year (in reality, the first eleven months for a deceased parent and the first thirty days for a deceased child, sibling, or spouse) to express their grief through praying the Mourners Kaddish on a daily basis. This daily spiritual practice supports the healing process by enabling mourners to remember the deceased, experience the joy and pain of the relationship, and adjust to the absence of the loved one.

For Christians and other spiritual seekers who choose not to practice a formal period of mourning, the healing process is facilitated by setting aside regular time for remembering and praying for the beloved; noting their absence at holidays; and telling stories about them to the younger generation. Even if our daily prayers and remembrances have little direct impact on the dead, they transform our relationship with our deceased loved ones as well as our surviving family members and friends. Through our prayers, we experience the healing of memories and the future hope that, in the mysteries of Divine love, we will encounter the holy essence of our friends and family in God's Holy Adventure beyond the grave.

### Communities of Care

The biblical notions of shalom and the body of Christ remind us that our lives are intimately connected with one another. As a child growing up in a Baptist home Bruce remembers singing:

> Blest be the tie that binds
> our hearts in Christian love:
> the fellowship of kindred minds
> is like to that above.[9]

In healthy communities, we celebrate each other's joys, support each other's projects, and mourn each other's losses. We learn the dynamic interplay of giving and receiving. When we are suffering, we let others comfort us. We break down the barriers of independence to open the doors to the healing waters of interdependence. When we openheartedly receive from others, our spirits are nurtured and empowered. We know that, despite the current agony we feel, we are going to make it because when we fall, there will always be someone to pick us up. Our receptivity to comfort and support enables our friends and family to share in the circle of healing by becoming givers themselves. Our receptivity also awakens their hearts to healthy and creative love.

In the ecology of life, we know that our pain and weakness will be the foundation of our caring for others. As he lived with a chronic illness that often required him to depend on the kindness of others, the Apostle Paul noted that in communion with God and other spiritual friends "whenever I am weak, then I am strong" (2 Cor. 12:10). Our growing sensitivity to the suffering of the world, and our appreciation for the gifts we have received in challenging times, will inspire us to complete the circle of healing by caring for others in similar crises.

## Spiritual Practices for Those Who Mourn

The healing path joins the inner journey of prayer and meditation with the outer journey of caring companionship. Spiritual practices radiate beyond our individual experience to raise the light of others as well as ourselves and awaken angels in the boulders of life. They may even play a supportive role in the afterlife adventures of our loved ones. Healing the grieving spirit involves cultivating practices such as imaginative prayer, thanksgiving, remembrance, forgiveness, affirmations, journaling, and other spiritual practices. (As in the case of all imaginative prayers, you can alter these in ways that suit you. Also, if your pain is too great, simply ask for God's healing presence in your life and seek the companionship of a friend, spiritual leader, or professional counselor.)

### *Healing through Prayerful Imagination*

Imaginative prayer heals mind, body, spirit, and relationships by enabling us to discover alternative ways of viewing our current life situation and by placing our lives in the context of God's lively companionship.

#### WALKING IN THE LIGHT OF GOD MEDITATION

As in the case of all imaginative prayers, we invite you to relax in a comfortable position as you let go of the stresses of the day. Place yourself in God's loving care, knowing that God is your companion in the valley of grief and growth. Take time to breathe gently and slowly, letting the radiant light of God fill your whole being. In the quiet, you may choose to reflect on the first words of Psalm 27: "[God] is my light and my salvation; whom shall I fear?"

Imagine yourself walking on a trail pathway, winding through a canyon. As you walk, you reflect on the loss of your loved one. What are your feelings? What challenges are facing you in the road that lies ahead? As you journey around each bend, what new threats are you experiencing? Imagine these threats externalized in the world as night begins to fall. How do you feel about walking in the darkness?

In the course of your walk, you discover that you are accompanied by a Being of Light, the Divine One. How do you feel in the companionship of the Divine One? The brightness of the Divine Light surrounds you and lights the path ahead. With God as your companion, what adventures await you? Amid the painful realities that may lie ahead, do you see any blessings?

In the distance, you see that the path leads to a gentle valley. What do you see on the horizon? Imagine the future that lies ahead with God as your companion. What hopes do you have in the Divine Presence?

As this meditation concludes, you hear God speaking to you. "I will be your guiding light and companion. Even when you don't see me, I will be here to protect and lead you." Conclude the meditation with the experience of being surrounded, permeated, and guided by the Faithful and Eternal Light.

### WITH CHRIST ON THE ROAD TO EMMAUS

Take time to read Luke 25:13–35. If you are not a Christian, think of your companion as the Loving God. Indeed, progressive Christianity sees the resurrection of Jesus as a global reality, not confined to Christianity, but embracing and transforming all persons in every age in their own unique personal and spiritual context.

As you reflect on a recent loss, you find yourself walking from the place of the funeral or memorial service to your home. You are accompanied by your most supportive companion on the journey back home. Take a moment to imagine the way home. What things will you see? Do you plan to stop along the way?

As you walk, you share your grief with one another. What things do you share with each other? You also share stories about the recently deceased one. What stories do you share?

Along your walk, you find yourself joined by a stranger. The stranger is vaguely familiar in appearance. Though you don't know him or her, you feel a great peace and comfort in his or her presence. He or she asks you how you are doing and without effort, you pour out your heart to the loving stranger. What things do you say? What is his or her response? How do you feel to share your heart with this "stranger?"

As you reach your home, you invite the stranger to dinner. He or she accepts your invitation and converses with you while you prepare the meal. What foods do you serve him or her?

Before you begin to eat, your new companion asks if he might pray. What words does he use in his prayer? As you listen, you slowly recognize that the stranger is Jesus, the Holy One, the Healing One of God. How do you feel at this recognition? As he completes the prayer, you notice that Jesus is gone. However, in his departure, he leaves a message: "I will always be with you. I am with your loved one, and I will guide her (or his) way." How do you feel when you hear these words?

Conclude with words of thanksgiving for God's presence even in the most difficult times. (You may also choose to focus on an encounter with God, an angelic being, or Divine Wisdom, rather than Jesus in this visualization.)

### SAYING GOOD-BYE

In this imaginative prayer, you find yourself with your recently deceased loved one at a place of departure—an air terminal, bus station, railroad station, or a fork in the road. Imagine the scene that surrounds you. In a few moments, he or she must leave you to begin the next stage of the spiritual journey. What words do you say to one another? What physical gestures do you make toward one another? How do you feel at this leave taking? Is there any unfinished business? (If so, simply share any final words in conversation with the other.) Are there any words of love or gratitude that you wish to share?

Now, it is time to say "good-bye." Two angelic beings appear beside you. What do they look like? What do they say to you?

One of them takes your beloved's hand and accompanies him or her to the place of departure. Your beloved is surrounded by angelic, loving light. Take time to see the light of God surrounding your beloved as he or she departs. Do you have any final words you wish to say before your beloved journeys to the next adventure?

The other being takes your hand as you wave good-bye. How do you feel to have this angelic being beside you? The meditation concludes with the angelic being returning home with you and promising to be your companion in the days ahead.

### Graceful Gratitude

Thanksgiving links the living and the dead and reminds us of the beauty and significance of our loved ones. In this exercise, we invite you to set aside several minutes each day for a week, simply to say "thank you." You may find yourself crying as you remember the wonder of your beloved, her or his utter uniqueness in your life. These are tears of celebration as well as grief.

You may do this spiritual exercise in many ways, alone or with friends and family. One way to get started is to use the pattern:

"I am thankful for _____." or "I thank you for _____" or

"I thank God for _____."

With each thanksgiving, you may choose to imagine a scene in which the beloved revealed these traits. For example, when Tom followed this exercise, his first response was "I am thankful for Dad's loving care when I was a child." He then remembered two scenes from his childhood: playing catch in the backyard with his father and reading books in the morning with his father. Sondra remembered how grateful she was for her mother's unconditional support. She remembered how her mother welcomed her home without judgment following her separation and divorce from her first husband. Sondra recounts, "I will never forget her complete acceptance. I knew that from her traditional background, divorce was difficult to affirm. But I felt that she understood why I had to leave and would support me, no matter what."

In order to ground your thanksgiving over the long haul, you may choose to create a gratitude journal in which you note the blessings you have received from the deceased's life, draw pictures, write poetry, and place photographs.

### *Remembering and Reconnecting*

Remembrance is at the heart of both Christianity and Judaism. At Passover, Jews experience the liberation from Egypt as a contemporary reality by telling the story of Moses and God's deliverance of the captives. In a similar fashion, when Christians celebrate Communion (also called Holy Eucharist, the Mass, or the Lord's Supper), they rehearse the ancient story of Jesus' last Passover supper with his disciples and experience Jesus as a living reality in the bread and the wine. As we remember our loved ones, we discover that, at a deep level, they live on in our lives. Their influence cannot be severed by death or distance. This exercise, which has many alternative styles, can be done individually or with family or loved ones.

You may choose to bring out old letters, memorabilia, photographs, or videos. Recall the events surrounding these "snapshots from life." How did you feel? What was special about that event? What did your loved one say? Relive the event from your current perspective, knowing that the past we retrieve is always conditioned by our feelings, thoughts, and experiences.

You may choose simply to let your mind wander or journal these events. If you are in a group, you may choose to share your various feelings and remembrances with your companions. This gathering can be a "remembrance party" in which you share favorite foods of the deceased (provided you enjoy them!) along with recollections, funny stories, and celebrating beverages.

### A FUNERAL JOURNAL

Many grievers have found the practice of keeping a funeral journal or scrapbook helpful in remembering the events immediately following the death of a loved one. Knowing the brevity of life, Liz chose to memorialize her parents' deaths by collecting cards, service bulletins, personal notes, and papers from the funeral home in an album. Along with these, she took time in the days following her respective parents' deaths to journal her feelings, to describe encounters, and to remember special moments in their relationship. From time to time, she looks back at her musings and memorabilia as a way of keeping her memories of these life-changing events alive. She also believes that her children will find these helpful in remembering their family history.

## Forgiveness and Letting Go

Virtually all of us have unfinished business with the deceased. These exercises enable us to experience our pain in light of God's healing love. In so doing, we participate in God's forgiveness. Even when we cannot forgive the other, God is working in our lives to bring healing and forgiveness.

### LETTING GO OF BURDENS

In this exercise, imagine yourself walking down a country road with a heavy backpack on your back. What is your environment? Where are you going? You notice the pack is heavy, weighed down by grievances and guilt. What things, in the relationship to the recently deceased, are unhealed or burdensome? Take a moment to feel the weight of these burdens. Notice how heavy they are.

You stop for a moment to rest and notice that you have a companion—the Being of Light and Love. This companion offers to carry the burdens for you. What is your decision? Do you want to hold on to the burdens or let them go?

If you wish to hold on to them, remember the weight of them upon your life.

If you wish to let go of your burdens, begin to take them one by one out from your backpack, examining each one, feeling each one, and then sharing them with the Being of Light and Love. Do you experience an angel in the burdens? How does it feel to let go of the burdens?

Now it is time to continue the journey. If you have let go of your burdens, feel the ease of walking now. Feel the joy of this Divine Lightness.

### CUTTING THE CORD

Some of the ties that bind the living and dead are painful and debilitating. Ironically, by cutting the cord of negativity, we can embrace the holiness of the deceased.

Take a few moments to relax in the companionship of the Holy One. Reflect on your relationship with the deceased. Is there any unfinished business? Are there any ties that bind you with the deceased, whose presence may interfere with the healing process? Notice these ties and explore their potential impact, positive and negative, on your life. Imagine these ties as a cord that binds both you and the deceased, preventing you from becoming the person God intends for you be. Feel the imprisoning aspects of this cord. Are you ready to let go and cut the cord?

The Holy One takes your hand and gives you a pair of scissors or a knife. You may choose to share these scissors, or the knife, with the deceased. Along with the Holy One, the two of you (or simply yourself alone) cut the cord, releasing both of you from the negative ties that bind. How does it feel to cut the cord? How does it feel to be free? Is there anything you wish to say to the Holy One or to the deceased? Take time to share your thoughts and feelings.

Conclude this exercise with a prayer of thanksgiving for God's companionship and your new freedom.

### FORGIVENESS MEDITATION

In the spirit of an earlier meditation in this book (pp. 40–41), we go back to a time in our lives with we have been hurt by the deceased. What moment was painful? Does it still subtly shape your life? How do you feel about this event today? Take some time to imagine the scene and how you felt at the time.

Now envisage the Being of Light and Love with you in the scene. Feel the comfort that comes from the Divine Presence. Share your feelings with the Divine. In the presence of God, share your feelings with the other. Experience yourself as safe and strong. Experience both yourself and the deceased enveloped in Divine Healing Light. Let the light transform the situation and its meaning in your life today. If possible, tell the deceased that you forgive her or him. If this is too difficult, place your unforgiveness in God's hands and let God heal both you and the deceased. Allow God to share the forgiveness that is not possible for you at this time.

Throughout this exercise, remember that you are completely safe in God's care. (If the emotional content of this exercise is too painful, simply conclude the exercise at any time and place your life in God's healing light. If you have experienced physical, sexual, or emotional abuse that is unresolved, we suggest that you defer this exercise until you perceive yourself to be on a healing path. We want to reaffirm the importance of psychotherapy, pastoral counseling, and spiritual direction in the healing process, especially when there has been physical, sexual, psychological, or narcissistic abuse.)

If you feel guilt about your relationship with the deceased, you may choose to follow this exercise from the perspective of one who needs forgiveness, either for something you have done or something you neglected to do. After you have discerned whether your feelings of guilt are justified—recognizing that you can feel guilty for events that were out of your control at the time—follow the previous exercise by inviting God to be your companion as you seek the forgiveness of the other. Remember that God is always ready to forgive us and to enable us to begin again as God's beloved companions in the mending of the world.

## *Healing Affirmations*

Affirmations transform our minds and our bodies. At life's most difficult moments when we are unsure if we can make it, affirmations remind us of an alternative reality in which we find strength to face our fears. Affirmations do not deny the grief and despair we feel, but place our deepest pain in a holy perspective. As we discover our inner strength, we can face our pain and anguish without denial, for we know that we are going to make it.

While affirmations are profoundly personal, the following scriptural and non-scriptural affirmations are helpful in times of loss:

God is with me in the darkest valley. (Ps. 23:4)

God is my light and my salvation; I will not be afraid. (Ps. 27:1)

God is my refuge and strength in this time of trouble. (Ps. 46:1)

God's light shines in the darkness, and this darkness cannot overcome it. (Jn. 1:5)

Nothing can separate me from the love of God. (Rom. 8:29)

God is with me in my pain and loss.

My loved one is in God's hands.

With God as my companion, I am being healed
every day.

With God as my companion, I will make it through
this grief.

I am never alone.

I have the resources to face each day.

In the long valley of grief, we are never alone. We always
have the resources of the Divine Companion, a healing
community of friends, and our own divinely-given inner
strength. We can experience healing because there is a force for
transformation and wholeness that is always at work even in our
grief. Each of us is stronger and more resourceful than we
imagine even in life's most painful moments; we can find angels
in life's most jagged boulders.

# CHAPTER SIX

# *Beauty in Boulders*

Our vocation in life involves finding and bringing forth angels in boulders. In Jewish mysticism, this task is called *tikkun,* the mending and healing of the world that occurs in the lives of individuals and communities.

Progressive Judaism and Christianity are hopeful about the human adventure. Despite the reality of death and grief on the personal level as well as injustice, violence, and ecological destruction on the national and global levels, progressive spirituality affirms the original wholeness of all things. The goodness of creation can be hidden, but it cannot be destroyed. Within the most challenging situations, there is an angelic reality poised to spring forth. Where the pain and injustice is greatest, there is also a gentle, persistent, and resourceful Power that seeks healing and transformation. The presence of this Holy Power, defined by love rather than coercion, gives us reason to be hopeful in life's challenging situations.

The reality of God does not eliminate the harsh realities of loss and pain. Divine Power and Love, from the very beginning, created a space for freedom and creativity. This freedom can bring forth beauty and kindness, but it can also bring forth the chaos of cancer, alcohol-related deaths, and unjust and dehumanizing political structures. In the face of the world's evils, on the individual and social levels, we are given the choice of life and death. We are given imaginative alternatives to the present pain and injustice. From his experiences during the Holocaust, Viktor Frankl notes that while we may lose every external freedom, we still have the freedom to choose our attitude toward the events of our lives.

In the face of death and grief, we may choose denial and passivity. However, we may also choose healing and transformation. *Denial* is real and sometimes life-supporting. We may need a moment to adjust physiologically and emotionally to unexpected tragedy.

Nevertheless, over the long haul, denial deadens the spirit, undermines relationships, and stifles creativity, because it blocks the wellsprings of healing. Just think of the isolation and anguish that lie just under the surface, when families live by a mutual charade of wellness and normalcy, when the signs of death are all around. One of the greatest insights of the biblical tradition is the ever-present recognition that healing comes from embracing pain, injustice, and death with God as our companion in the struggle.

Overwhelmed by life's tragedies, we may also take the path of *passivity*. On this path, only the jagged and ugly boulder is real, only sickness and death have power. Death becomes the god that defines the realm of possibility for ourselves and our loved ones. We see ourselves entirely in terms of our illness and forget the resources for change that are always at our disposal. When boulders block the path to the future, we simply give up rather than exploring alternate routes. There is, however, more to reality, ourselves, and Divine possibility than we often recognize. The angel rolls away the stone on Easter morning. The Holy God of Israel parts the sea and creates a pathway to freedom.

The way of *healing and transformation* is the path of stature and hope. In embracing the fullness of life, we experience the suffering of the world and our own despair and grief. Nevertheless, we also experience our original wholeness as God's children and the spaciousness of a heart equally open to the pain and joy of the world. Through prayer, meditation, and holy relationships, we discover that we are not alone in dying and grieving. The Holy One is our companion. For those with open spirits, God is constantly at work to bring persons and events into our lives that will promote our healing and wellness. Living and dying alike can reveal the Beauty that is God's aim for the universe.

In the path of healing and transformation, we become the artists of our own experience and co-creators with God and our fellow humans. Out of the complexities of experience, we create a life of beauty—open to tragedy broken dreams, well aware of the brevity of life, but equally open the wonder of each creature and our own responsibility to heal the world by healing ourselves and our immediate environment. No longer imprisoned by our own pain and self-centeredness, we identify our well being with the wholeness of the planet and God's aims for our lives and the world. As our spirits grow in stature, we creatively synthesize hope and fear, pain and joy, beauty and chaos.

Open to the world in its many dimensions, we recognize the importance of communities of care. God's aim at shalom inspires us to choose abundant life in our families, work places, houses of worship, and communities. The healing of the world, including the comforting of the dying and bereaved, involves creating environments where wholeness is the norm— where the hungry are fed, the oppressed liberated, and the weapons of war dismantled.

Progressive Christian and Jewish spirituality is ultimately hopeful because we share our healing journey with God. The suffering servant of Israel and the one on the cross redefine our understandings of Divine Power and Presence. God is "the great companion—the fellow sufferer who understands," but God is also the ever-present force for healing and change—not just for ourselves but also for all creation.[1]

God is on our side. Our lives spring from Divine Creativity and find their ultimate completion and transformation in the Holy Adventure of God's memory and creative love.

Grateful for the wonder of our being, regardless of our life situation, we can find angels in boulders. Even when death is on horizon, we can trust God's healing artistry as we proclaim with Dag Hammarskjold:

"Night is drawing nigh—"
For all that has been—Thanks!
To all that shall be—Yes![2]

# Notes

## Chapter 1: Finding Angels in Boulders

[1]We have articulated the foundations of a progressive Jewish and Christian spirituality in our previous books, *Mending the World: Spiritual Hope for Ourselves and Our Planet* (Philadelphia: Innisfree, 2002) and *Walking in the Light: A Jewish-Christian Vision of Healing and Wholeness* (St. Louis: Chalice Press, 2004).

[2]Martin Buber, *Tales of the Hasidim: The Early Masters* (New York: Schocken, 1947), 11.

## Chapter 2: Adventures in Immortality

[1]Raymond Moody, *Life After Life* (New York: Bantam, 1976) and Betty Eadie, *Embraced by the Light* (Placerville, Calif.: Gold Leaf Press, 1992).

[2]Brian Weiss, *Many Lives, Many Masters* (New York: Simon and Schuster, 1988).

[3]Martin Buber, *Tales of the Hasidim: The Later Masters,* trans. Olga Marx (New York: Schocken, 1948), 249–50.

[4]Abraham Joshua Heschel, *I Asked for Wonder* (New York: Crossroad, 1983), 71–72.

[5]For an extended discussion of Christian understandings of reincarnation, see Bruce G. Epperly, *Crystal and Cross* (St. Louis: Chalice Press, 1996).

[6]For an extended discussion of Jewish images of death and immortality, see Lewis Solomon, *Jewish Spirituality: Revitalizing Judaism for the Twenty First Century* (Northdale, N.J.: Jason Aronson, 2000).

[7]Moody, *Life After Life,* 64–66.

## Chapter 3: Healing the Dying

[1]Adapted from Joseph Hertz, *The Authorized Daily Prayer Book,* rev. ed. (New York: Bloch, 1985), 105.

[2]Adapted from Matthew and Dennis Linn, *Healing Life's Hurts* (New York: Paulist Press, 1978 and 1984).

[3]Mitch Albom, *Tuesdays with Morrie* (New York: Doubleday, 1997), 174–75.

[4]Simone de Beauvoir, *A Very Easy Death* (New York: Warner Books, 1964), 93.

## Chapter 4: Living through Loss

[1]C. S. Lewis, *A Grief Observed* (New York: Bantam, 1976), 69.

[2]Ibid., 14.

[3]Ibid., 58–59.

[4]Ibid., 4–5.

[5]For more extended discussions of bereavement, we suggest Victor Parachin *Grief Relief* (St. Louis: Chalice Press, 1991) and *Healing Grief* (St. Louis: Chalice Press, 2001); Jerroid O'Neil Roussel, *Dealing with Grief: Theirs and Ours* (New York: Alba House, 1999); Granger Westberg, *Good Grief* (Minneapolis: Fortress Press, 1979).

[6]Lewis, *A Grief Observed,* 5–6.

## Chapter 5: Mending the Broken Connection

[1]John Newton, "Amazing Grace," 1779.

[2]Joseph H. Hertz, *The Authorized Daily Prayer Book,* rev. ed. (New York: Bloch, 1985), 270.

[3]C. S. Lewis, *A Grief Observed* (New York: Bantam, 1976), 58–59.

[4]The term "thin place" emerged from the Celtic tradition to describe the intersection of God and the world, and time and eternity. Traditionally, thin places have been places of revelation and dynamic energy, such as Jerusalem, Sinai, and Mecca. Today, Iona, Scotland; Glastonbury, England; and Sedona, Arizona, have been described as thin places by spiritual seekers.

[5]*Book of Worship, United Church of Church* (New York: Office of Church Life and Leadership, 1986), 372.

[6]Hertz, *Authorized Prayer Book,* 1073.

[7]Adapted from the Central Conference of American Rabbis, *Gates of Prayer: The New Union Prayer Book* (New York: Central Conference of American Rabbis, 1975), 629–30.

[8]*Book of Worship, United Church of Christ,* 381.

[9]Words by John Fawcett, 1872, from "Blest Be the Tie That Binds."

## Chapter 6: Beauty in Boulders

[1]Alfred North Whitehead, *Process and Reality: Corrected Edition* (New York: Free Press, 1978), 351.

[2]Dag Hammarskjold, *Markings* (New York: Alfred A. Knopf, 1964), 89.